GEMINI

22 MAY - 21 JUNE

First published in Australia and New Zealand in 2005
by Harlequin Enterprises Pty Ltd.

ABN 47 001 180 918

3 Gibbes Street, Chatswood, NSW 2067 AUSTRALIA.

ISBN 0 733 56374 0

Typeset at Anthony Bushelle Graphics by Robert Muzic
Designed by Sarah Bull

Printed and bound in Australia by McPhersons Printing Group

ABOUT
DADHICHI

Dadhichi is one of Australia's foremost astrologers, frequently seen on TV and in the media. He has the unique ability of drawing from complex astrological theory to provide clear, easily understandable advice and insights for people who want a reliable indication of what their future may hold.

In the 23 years that Dadhichi has been practising astrology, face reading and other esoteric studies, he has conducted over 8,000 consultations. His clients include celebrities, political and diplomatic figures and media and corporate identities from all over the world.

Dadhichi's unique blend of astrology and face reading assists people in fulfilling their true potential. His extensive experience practising western astrology is complemented by his research into the theory and practice of eastern forms of astrology.

Dadhichi has been a guest on Australia's leading television networks, on which several of his political and worldwide forecasts have proved to be uncannily accurate. He appears regularly on Channel 9's *Mornings with Kerri Anne* and is a weekly columnist for *Woman's Day* magazine.

His websites www.astrology.com.au and www.facereader.com attract hundreds of thousands of visitors each month and offer a wide variety of features, helpful information and services.

Dedicated to The Light of Intuition
Sri V. Krishnaswamy – Mentor and Friend

With thanks to Julie, Joram, Isaac and Janelle

CONTENTS

THE
GEMINI
IDENTITY

GEMINI AT A GLANCE

KEY CHARACTERISTICS
Versatile, intellectual, communicative, social, has many interests, loves variety and change

COMPATIBLE STAR SIGNS
Aries, Leo, Libra, Sagittarius, Aquarius

KEY LIFE PHRASE
I Think

ZODIAC TOTEM
The Twins

ZODIAC SYMBOL
♊

ZODIAC FACTS
Third sign of the zodiac, mutable, masculine and positive, barren

ELEMENT
Air

FAMOUS GEMINIS
Drew Carey, Bob Dylan, Anne Heche, Mike Myers, Miles Davis, Helena Bonham-Carter, Lenny Kravitz, Stevie Nicks, Gladys Knight, Kylie Minogue, Annette Benning, John F. Kennedy, Clint Eastwood, Brooke Shields, Marilyn Monroe, Mark Wahlberg, Prince, Anna Kournakova, Gene Wilder, Boy George, Paula Abdul, Paul McCartney, Venus Williams, Johnny Depp

The third sector of the zodiac reflects the principles of intelligence and communication—the way people express themselves. Being born under the third sign of the zodiac brings to the fore these attributes of intellectual expression within you. Gemini is a versatile sign and is found to take an interest in many different facets of life. If you could be accused of anything, it would be that your interests are so diverse you're sometimes superficial, taking a bit of this and a bit of that and not deepening your knowledge of the subject in question. Likewise, many Geminis are quite high-strung and tend to spread themselves very thin, taking on too much and not completing what they begin. Nevertheless, people love your company and this adaptability in your nature is what makes you interesting to others. You have an incredible breadth of knowledge and are able to talk to almost anyone about many differing views and the experiences you may have had. Communication is your Number One asset.

You have a wonderful love of the written word, as well as the spoken, and will often find yourself putting pen to paper and doodling your thoughts, if only to give you an insight into your own thinking processes. Many journalists, writers and other advisers are born under the sign of Gemini; their forte with words makes a lasting impression.

The third sign of Gemini also relates to travels and short journeys. As a Gemini you'll find yourself restless on many occasions and your itchy feet will cause you to travel frequently. These journeys may not always be long, but you are always on the go. You thirst for new experiences. Even on short journeys and in transit, you are the sort of person who would love to meet new people and share your ideas—even with perfect strangers. You're fascinated by the way the human mind works and the way people interact generally. Again, you must curb the tendency towards frivolous mental activity and excessive thought, because your mental efforts could, from time to time, cause you exhaustion.

You can't handle close-mindedness of any sort. With your inquisitive and restless mind you have an eclectic taste, having dabbled in many different viewpoints and topics. You're aware of the different types of personalities in life and are, therefore, liberal and free-thinking in your approach.

Geminis seem to grow younger rather than older with age. Your physical appearance will maintain that youthful glow and you will continue to exhibit a fun-loving energy. Along with this youthful exuberance, you exhibit a sharp wit that enhances your communications. This will definitely make you the favourite among your peers.

GEMINI WOMAN

As a typical Gemini woman is usually tall, slender and very attractive to look at, you will have no problems attracting the opposite sex. Slenderness may be more predominant if you're born in the second half of Gemini. Those born in the earlier part, particularly nearer the time of Taurus, may have a slightly more curvaceous and fleshy body. The emotional and sensual aspects of Venus will be very strong.

The mind of the Gemini woman is deep, and thoughtfully provocative. This being so, you need someone who can stimulate your intellectual needs as you have little respect for those who do not use their heads. You're ambitious and like to feel as though you've contributed something to your world, particularly in your social and professional arena. Because of Neptune ruling your career house, most people don't realise your softer, sensuous and compassionate side, which is always available to give needed assistance when called upon. You are a caring individual, not just a 'thinker'.

You need to be careful not to overreact to the statements of others. This is because your basic nature is curious, inquisitive and ready for an intellectual challenge. You can usually spot a fake and have no fear in expressing the truth in response to others. You can, however, be hypersensitive and jump to conclusions. By curbing these qualities you'll make an ideal friend and lover and can be proud of your intellectual achievements.

GEMINI MAN

The Gemini male is usually tall and in some cases, especially if born in the earlier part of Gemini, can be muscular. As a Gemini male you are always on the go and tend to be busier than most. In relationships this could make you the proverbial "rolling stone that gathers no moss".

You may find it difficult to commit due to your intense work agenda, but also to your finicky nature when it comes to finding someone who meets all your criteria. You do have very high expectations of all your friends and associates, and more so with the lovers you choose.

If you engage in friendship and partnerships of a romantic nature, it may be noted that you're quite restless, fidgety and at times even inattentive, due to your preoccupation with the many things you feel you must achieve. If you're on the lookout to meet the right person, fewer words may at times be of benefit to you. Your persuasive and strong storytelling style can fascinate others, but you must learn to note non-verbal communication signals when people become a little overwhelmed by your intellectual passion.

The Mars rulership of your friendship sector indicates your loyalty as a friend and your dynamic energy and speed in responding to the needs of anyone you consider a friend. You'll always be there to help them and can offer great advice, even sacrificing your own time to assist them in achieving their ends. The other side of the coin is that you are also most adept at recognising opportunities and are quite an entrepreneurial character.

GEMINI CHILD

Your Gemini child is a curious creature of the zodiac, having a well-developed intellectual response to everything around him or her. From the earliest age Geminis are inquisitive and will constantly keep you on your toes with a myriad of questions about matters you won't have answers for.

Ruled by Mercury, the little Gemini character is full of mirth, fun and practical jokes as well. You'll never be able to shut them up, as communication is not only the best way for them to articulate their thinking, but it also lets off a lot of the nervous energy that is part of their character, even from their earliest years. Because of this you will need to quickly engage your child in activities that can fruitfully utilise their busy little brains.

To keep your Gemini child healthy it is a great idea to feed them regularly with a good variety of fruits and vegetables and with lean low-fat protein to give their little systems something to anchor them. If you do this, your Gemini child will maintain optimum levels of energy, physically and mentally, to perform well at school. Your Gemini child will be bright and excel well at school, but as with the typical Gemini adult, a valuable lesson is to tackle one task at a time, rather than skimming the surface and attempting too many things simultaneously. Gemini children enjoy subjects that involve problem-solving and mental deduction. Maths, science, communication skills, writing, singing and music are also areas in which they can excel.

Puberty is the critical time in which their scattered energies may get the better of them. They may overstep the bounds of their own mental and physical capability to handle life and may invite difficulties, through poor judgment of peers. Your wise counsel will be essential in these formative years so that your Gemini child can grow into a fully integrated and productive member of society.

ROMANCE, LOVE AND MARRIAGE

You are dominated by your intellectual processes in your search for the perfect soul mate. Your idealistic nature is constantly on the lookout for the supremely better mate who can fulfil all your wildest imaginations. You have a busy social agenda and are quick to make friends and feel initially that "yes this is the one". But you'll soon learn that love is not a matter of an intellectual process or a deduction about character, strengths or personality flaws. The challenge for you is to experience love on an emotional level, in which you can "feel" the other person's heart and soul.

You are somewhat cynical and critical. This is the reason some of your relationships do not last long. You must learn to give people scope for their own development and not be too harsh on them as we are all prone to human frailties.

In marriage you need to connect with one who can meet you on an equal footing intellectually. Being able to share your thoughts is important in a mate. If you meet someone who has an emotional perspective, you may be challenged by them. Finding the happy medium will be a struggle until you learn to sink your mind into your heart and surrender to the flow of your feelings.

As a Gemini you can have a fruitful marriage. At some point, after your smorgasbord-style relationships, you will find a suitable mate who will be noble, kind and endearing, as well as generous. Friends will not always support you and you should factor time alone, because on occasion differences of opinion and even out-right fights may ensue. Overall, your marriage factors indicate a favourable outcome and destiny in your relationship affairs, once you overcome this mental aspect of your nature.

HEALTH AND VITALITY

You're constantly on the move and this is because your ruling planet Mercury represents the winged messenger of speed, grace and versatility. Take care not to run yourself into the ground as your energy levels are completely dependent on the wellbeing of your nervous system. Ordinarily, you have strong health and good vitality, but you do tend to live on your nerves.

Because you take on too many projects simultaneously, you're constantly rushing to meet your deadlines. Haste and impulse may also cause you problems in terms of mishaps, accidents and other unwanted physical stress. By managing your time, eating smaller meals and doing so in an environment that is conducive to increasing your wellbeing, you'll overcome many of the problems associated with your star sign.

Your airways, lungs, shoulders, arms and hands are all dominated by Gemini. Keeping yourself warm and avoiding draughts, especially in the winter months, will ensure you don't fall prey to bronchitis, asthma and other pulmonary problems.

DIET

Avoid foods that produce excess gas and are not tolerated by the digestive system. The importance of attention to food combinations cannot be overestimated. Eat more slowly and talk less while eating. Because you love social discourse it's hard for you to simply remain silent while chewing your food. Most foods will agree with you if only you'd learn the cardinal rule for Gemini: moderately eat smaller meals more frequently throughout the day to adequately nourish your overburdened nervous system.

Try to cook and eat in an environment conducive to harmony. Lean high-protein foods are excellent to give you the energy to sustain you throughout the day. Oats and other raw grains and muesli first thing in the day are perfect staple diets for the Gemini character.

PROFESSION AND CAREER

Because Mercury, your ruler, is an intellectual and analytical planet, you need to use your mind and rational powers to give you a sense of satisfaction in your work. Having great powers of oratory will give you the opportunity to make your mark in the world through your speech and also the written word. Yet, later on in life, many Geminis find that the Pisces influence on their career sectors steers them towards more humanitarian activities, as the nature of Neptune and Jupiter is rather spiritual.

Many Geminis job-hop for quite a few years before actually settling down into the profession they feel suits their temperament and their idealistic views of what work means to them. Often they are capable of conducting more than one activity or profession at once. Your love of variety will always have you moving from one interest to another.

You love to diligently collate and manage facts and figures and are therefore a reliable person when it comes to handling the detail work in any business. You're not scared to attempt things you haven't tried before, but you do have a tendency to be a little overconfident in matters of which you have little experience. If that happens, don't be afraid to elicit the assistance of someone more experienced or wiser. Accounting, bookkeeping, computers, sales work, public relations, advertising, teaching, secretarial, travel industry and even editorial and journalistic professions are ideal avenues for your quick-witted Gemini mind.

KARMA AND SPIRITUALITY

The ninth sector of your horoscope is about your past life, Gemini, and in your case that area is ruled by Aquarius and the planets Uranus and Saturn. Because of this, your past life was progressive and intellectually very demanding. In this present life, you've adopted many of those past intellectual traits that have made you forceful, dynamic and very powerful and persuasive in your communications. If you've learned the lessons of this last life, you will understand that intellectual arrogance and snobbery are the sorts of character traits others don't tolerate well. Unfortunately, some of the lesser-evolved Geminis have not grasped this most important facet of their spiritual development.

The more evolved types—and hopefully you fall into this category—have learned the lesson of sharing their intellectual blessings and have learned that true intellectual greatness is a continuing pathway, an adventure of learning and sharing. In this case you'll be an eternal student looking to further your intellectual horizons through many different studies, even in your advanced age. In fact, due to your past karma, you have an innate sense of childlike innocence and don't ever quite feel as though you've aged, irrespective of your physical age.

In your current lifetime, and your future life, your fifth sector indicates the karma and destiny you can expect and this is ruled by Venus and Libra, showing your social interests. Hopefully, you will not let this aspect of your nature, which is somewhat sensual, dominate your more intellectual and discriminative faculties this time around.

EMOTIONAL BALANCE

The quality of air predominates in the Gemini temperament and this relates to the nervous system, lungs and brain processes. The pattern of breathing will be intimately linked to your mental and emotional equilibrium, in fact, all of your biophysical processes, Gemini. To gain emotional balance it is most important for you to begin regulating your breathing and to lessen the level of excitement in your life. This will produce calm and tranquillity, thus enabling you to utilise your talents to the fullest.

Other methods of balancing yourself spiritually and emotionally include the use of gems and metals. Your lucky gem is a green emerald, and silver or gold are useful metals to tap the energies of Mercury and the Sun. Essential oils of sandalwood, Himalayan cedar wood, pine and ylang ylang will soothe your speedy and overly busy nature.

FINANCIAL LUCK AND SUCCESS

A high-quality, flawless emerald should be set in a silver or gold ring, with the gem touching either your third finger, that is, your ring finger, or little finger. Ideally these gems should be set in the ring on a Wednesday during the waxing Moon to tap the powerful energies of your ruling planet Mercury. This will give wonderful calmness to your physical and mental selves and bring you good luck generally. For personal success, Wednesday and Friday are your luckiest days.

CAREER LUCK AND ADVANCEMENT

Utilising the gems of green emerald, green tourmaline, peridot or jade will ensure lucky breaks in respect of your professional or career path. If you are considering a job interview or some other important meeting, Wednesdays and Fridays will provide you with the right sort of windows of opportunity. The other lucky gem for you is blue sapphire or amethyst. The combination of blue sapphire and diamond is an especially lucky one for you.

MARRIAGE AND ROMANCE

To speed up your luck in meeting members of the opposite sex and to also bring peace and harmony into your domestic sphere, particularly with your children, using white coral or diamond will be specifically lucky for you karmically. You should wear these gems on the second finger of the right or left hand and ideally they should be set in silver or platinum. To pacify your own emotions, setting the diamond on a Friday will be especially powerful and can attract those planetary powers that will bring you the romantic and family luck you so desire.

LUCKY COLOURS

Bottle-green, apple-green, cream, white and blue are especially lucky for you. Navy blue and cream, as a combination, is lucky to advance your professional and personal agendas.

LUCKY DAYS

Your luckiest days are Wednesday, Friday and Saturday, being ruled by the planets that are most friendly to you.

LUCKY NUMBERS AND LOTTO

The following are your lucky numbers, Gemini. Try exploring their value when embarking on any gambling or purchasing of lottery tickets, bearing in mind that your lucky days, lucky colours and, of course, the forecasts and other advice given later in this book will help to optimise your chance of winning.

5, 14, 23, 32, 41

8, 17, 26, 35, 44

6, 15, 24, 33, 42

YOUR DESTINY YEARS

Your most important years are as follows: 5, 14, 23, 32, 41, 50, 68, 77, 86.

HEALING AND MEDITATION

Because of your restless mind it would be advisable to draw the energies of Saturn, your ninth ruler of spirituality. The day of Saturn is Saturday and by meditation, prayer and other personal rituals on that day you can strongly appease the negative karmas associated with your planets. This will help accelerate your spiritual evolution. Spend some time on a Saturday, at least drawing in the vibrations of the powerful and concentrated planet of Saturn. You can also meditate on Wednesday, Friday, new Moon, full Moon and eclipse days, which can draw your mind to that spiritually powerful area within your nature.

STAR SIGN
COMPATIBILITY

Astrologers believe that certain star signs are more compatible with certain other star signs. In this section we'll not only analyse the compatibility of your star sign with the other eleven signs but also study in more detail which time periods of each star sign are better suited to you. By doing so, we don't altogether dismiss a whole star sign as incompatible, for this wouldn't reflect the truth of love. In fact, with effort and compromise even the most difficult 'astrological' matches may have something to offer you. Don't close your mind to the beauty of life's possibilities!

Each combination includes an elemental match and result for quick and easy reference, for example, Aries is a fire sign and Aquarius an air sign. This combination produces a lot of "hot air". Air feeds fire and fire warms air. In fact, fire requires air. Interestingly, not all air and fire combinations work and this is where the fine-tuning of the specific birth periods within each star sign can be of assistance. Use the following headings for snippets of information to help you in understanding the elemental variety and nature of the star signs involved.

Even without the consideration of the love planets Venus and Mars, we are able to gain a good general understanding of your romantic prospects with other star signs. The Sun sign compatibility goes a long way in describing the essential qualities of a match and the character traits of both of you. Good luck in your search for love and may the stars shine upon you in 2006!

Gemini + Gemini   Air + Air = Wind

Fortunately you enjoy communication and so does your Gemini partner, who will satisfy you in full measure in this respect. You'll spend hours communicating and sharing ideas, telling jokes and generally enjoying each other's company, either together or in a social framework. You'll like the fact the Gemini you have attracted not only communicates but also is capable of intellectually absorbing ideas of a high order and reciprocating with concepts that stimulate your own creativity and idealism.

The weakness in this relationship stems from the fact that Gemini, being a mutable Air sign, gives very little grounding to the relationship and requires at least one of you to anchor the other. Both of you have the tendency to superficially skim the surface of topics, preferring a great deal of variety, rather than settling down and fully completing one task. If you're looking for a continuing relationship, the issues of money, stability and security may not be the issues you prefer to address, but it's imperative for two social butterflies such as yourselves to give these matters due consideration. It's essential for you to get in touch with your emotional nature. This is due to the fact that an imbalance in your intellectual natures obstructs you from getting in touch with each other at the heart level.

The relationship can be very playful on a sexual level, but this childlike innocence can only last if you consider a more meaningful and committed relationship with each other. Do give some careful consideration to these issues, as neither of you is capable of following through on many of your ideas, and marriage, for example, is one such commitment that requires tenacity and determination from the two of you.

Select those Geminis born between 22 May and 1 June; they possess good mental, social and communicational rapport with you. Geminis born between 2 and 12 June will be more sensual and are far better suited to an emotional and physical involvement. Those Geminis born between 13 and 21 June are more prone to be associated with you on a mental or spiritual level and could help resolve some of your karmic issues (or bring them to the fore in full measure).

Gemini + Cancer   Air + Water = Rain

As Cancer is a thoroughly sensitive and emotional sign, being ruled by the Moon, you may often feel at odds with why they feel the way they do. You are a more intellectual and thoughtful person, living in the realm of your head rather than your heart.

Conversely Cancer doesn't quite understand why you don't feel what they feel. There is an obvious gap between your essential natures and this will most definitely have to be bridged before any progress can be made in a relationship between you. Maybe it's simply a matter of accepting each other's vastly different character and the different roles you naturally play. This could work by delegating to each other tasks requiring these different talents of your personalities, that is, feeling and reasoning. If you try this the relationship may stand a chance of enduring.

Physically you may still find it difficult to bring your mind to a less rational means of relating to the Cancerian. Cancer wants to know that you want to feel and associate with their feelings, but this may be all too hard for you, as you love to think and talk about your thoughts in the bedroom. If Cancer won't reciprocate, you may regard this as a rebuttal of your intellectual worthiness. Remember, Gemini, there are non-verbal means of communicating and Cancer may just be the star to teach you a new level of understanding. Though not a perfect match, you can learn much from each other.

Cancerians born between 22 June and 3 July are linked to you financially, but may not offer you the emotional fulfilment you pine for. Cancerians born between 4 and 13 July may be too intense for you and squabbles could erupt just when you thought things were going your way. Those individuals of Cancer born between 14 and 23 July are a little less difficult to handle and high-quality friendships have been known to evolve from this partnership. Generally, you'll be able to quietly help develop the mental skills of Cancer, while they in turn teach you the secrets of getting in touch with your inner emotional self.

Gemini + Leo   Air + Fire = Hot Air

Because you are essentially an intellectual person possessing articulate, mental versatility, this ability will fan the flames of Leo's fiery pride. Leo will find you a most stimulating friend and companion and this works quite well, as Gemini falls in the sector of friendship to Leo. Gemini can indeed satisfy the social, intellectual and, to a certain extent, the emotional needs of Leo. Because Leo likes to dominate a situation, their personality comes on a little strong and you could find yourself one-upping each other in the attention-seeking stakes. In this sense, if you're both able to give and take by respecting each other's need to be centre stage, you'll complement each other well and satisfy each other on many levels of being.

The warm and enthusiastic fire of Leo will certainly stimulate you and give you the sense that your skills and talents are appreciated. Again, this is best expressed by both of you in a social context, as both Gemini and Leo love the company of others.

Leos tend to be hard taskmasters, fixed in their ideas, and therefore inflexible in their opinions. You on the other hand, Gemini, are more adaptable and less likely to stick to an inflexible viewpoint just for the sake of it (even though you don't mind the odd debate now and then).

In matters of love and affection both Gemini and Leo experience special moments of unbridled passion, which can produce some exciting and memorable experiences for both of you. This partnership could work well and indeed has a high chance of succeeding. You have middling results with Leos born 23 July to 4 August. Challenging and combative episodes are destined with those born between 15 and 23 August. If you're looking for a mate in the Leo clan, you're advised to prefer those born between 5 and 14 August.

Gemini + Virgo   Air + Earth = Dust

There are some intrinsic differences between Gemini and Virgo, notwithstanding their common rulership by Mercury. You sense many similarities in the Virgo temperament but may feel exasperated with their perfectionist attitude and orientation towards detail. You probably enjoy thinking, and playing mental games of communication with each other, but you, Gemini, are more likely to skim the surface of topics rather than submerge yourself too deeply in the minutiae, which is what Virgo prefers.

Virgo is the fourth sign to Gemini and points to your domestic and family sphere. Virgo will actually provide you with a safe haven from which to conduct the various activities that seem to be part of your world. You'll feel more anchored with Virgo, as they are an earth sign and can give you the sense of security and financial stability that you sometimes lack. There are some positive elements that connect the two of you, but you have a tendency to be a little more light-hearted and jocular about life. This could be cause for concern in the Virgo mind, which likes to see things from a more serious and virginal point of view. You must never offend the Virgo sensibilities as innocent as your jokes may appear. Virgo would do well to imbibe some of the softer and lighter attitude of Gemini, if only to make the path of life a little more enjoyable and less serious.

On the lovemaking side of things Virgo is somewhat more conservative, with Saturn ruling their sexual nature. Gemini and its Venus-ruled sexual sector of Libra is much more sensual and playful. This is probably not the greatest match between zodiac signs, but still has several redeeming factors and could be well worth a try. You have extremely good interactions with those Virgos born between 24 August and 2 September, due to Mercury's co-rulership. This is your own ruler. Those born between 13 and 23 September are co-ruled by Venus, also a cooperative planet promising many good times. Those Virgos born between 3 and 12 September will have deeply strong spiritual connections and will be wonderful advisers to you.

Gemini + Libra   Air + Air = Wind
This combination of air signs is most stimulating and likely to be a very good match in the long run. Venus and Mercury rule Libra

and Gemini respectively and are intimate planetary friends. The old dictum, 'as above, so below', means that you and Libra may develop this friendship into something quite special. The Libran will feel stimulated by your intellectual input and may even see you as some type of guru in educational matters or issues generally. On the other hand, Gemini, you may see Libra as the perfect lover, because this is the fifth or romantic sector for you. You could explore your social life to the fullest with each other and will spend many gratifying times in the company of friends and in artistic surroundings. You probably both enjoy live theatre, if not actively dabbling in the arts. Even though Gemini likes to race around doing a million and one things, Libra enjoys the stimulating activity and restlessness of the Gemini rapidity. Neither of you will feel contented "doing nothing" but that's not to say you won't enjoy sitting down in front of the fire, reading a good book together, and sipping hot chocolate on a cold winter's night. All in all, the relationship between Gemini and Libra is extremely well suited, not just intellectually but sexually. Both of you can find comfort, warmth and reciprocal love in this relationship. It is a combination that should be viewed as a lucky one.

An excellent love combination can be expected with those Librans born between 24 September and 3 October, as Venus, the co-ruler, offers you much love, warmth and affection. Librans born between 4 and 13 October are electric and stimulate your desire for change and novelty. There may be some difficulty settling down into any meaningful routine with them, though. Another great combination is with those Librans born between 14 and 23 October. You may well have excitement, but can feel a little more grounded with Librans of this type.

Gemini + Scorpio   Air + Water = Rain

Gemini, prepare yourself for the intensity of Scorpio on every level of your being! You are light-hearted, frivolous and although intellectual, may meet your match in the depth and radically transformative mind of Scorpio. While Gemini enjoys the discussion of a multitude of different topics, Scorpio is not content to skim the surface and simply sit around in idle discussion. There must be a deeper significance to these interactions and this could seem all too hot and heavy for you, Gemini. The planets ruling Gemini and Scorpio are Mercury and Pluto, with Mars exercising control over the intense Scorpio nature. These planets are not altogether easily reconciled and Scorpio may use this facet of in-depth psychic power to grill you, Gemini. This could cause some uneasiness in the relationship, but if you're prepared to learn from the probing relentless Scorpio, you may find aspects of your nature revealed that were hitherto hidden from you.

The interesting thing with this combination is that with the right focus and combination of your forces, there could well be some positive business and financial successes for the two of you. Gemini can coax Scorpio out of that unyielding, inflexible position to see a brighter and breezier aspect of the situation and even of life itself. However, the hastily spoken and at times frivolous Gemini could start to exasperate the Scorpio nerve and this is not a particularly strong enough bond to keep your relationship going.

Sexually, Scorpio will surprise you, Gemini, but you may feel as though Scorpio tries to dominate and control you. There is much seduction between these two signs, however, with the more powerful being Scorpio, who demands a deeper, less superficial relationship. Scorpio's possessiveness and jealousy won't sit well with your light-hearted and socially adaptable ways. You'll find it extremely difficult to see eye to eye with Scorpios born between 24 October and 2 November. There may be mutual respect but, at the end of the day, your opinions will differ vastly. Those Scorpios born between 13 and 22 November are far too emotional, and your intellect will not connect with them. Those born between 3 and 12 November are probably better suited to a lasting relationship or professional association.

Gemini + Sagittarius   Air + Fire = Hot Air

This combination of planetary energies is most fascinating indeed. Sagittarius happens to be the seventh sign to you, Gemini, and is ordinarily considered a great match, being the opposite sign of the zodiac. This is true and yet not so true, depending on which perspective you take. Both of you are mutable signs, meaning considerable change and variety are essential to your healthy mental and emotional states, but Gemini is more socially orientated than Sagittarius, who prefers a philosophical and idealistic view of life. Travel would ideally suit both of you and give you the chance, individually, as well as jointly, to experience these two seemingly diametric facets of your lives. The cultural and philosophical fascination of the Sagittarian and the social interaction of Gemini would find a perfect meeting point in this arena.

The seventh sector is the marriage sector, so it won't come as any surprise if both of you happened to cross each other's paths karmically to experience a magical interplay of planetary energies. The distinct differences require a lot of work by you both, though. If you can allow each other the freedom to explore and deepen your individual lives, your love can grow and develop into a relationship that you'll both feel comfortable with. Sexually there is good energy between the two of you, with the warm and endearing Sagittarian vibration stimulating your already intellectual and communicative style. This can be a great combination, or conversely, quite difficult.

A fine amalgamation of energies will be experienced if you team up with Sagittarians born between 23 November and 1 December. The reason is Jupiter's co-rulership, which has influence over your marital affairs. The experience with those Sagittarians born between 2 and 11 December is somewhat harrowing and does not suit your temperament easily, due to the Mars co-rulership. Those born between 12 and 22 December offer you mental stimulation, friendship and pleasurable pursuits. You'll consider these people as endearing friends.

Capricorn will immediately seem to drag Gemini's light and airy energy earthward and this grounding may not sit well with you, Gemini. With the exception of the business or professional dimension, this connection doesn't seem to really offer you much in the way of common interests or similar personality traits. This is because Capricorn happens to be the eighth or difficult sector for Gemini and reflects a strong karmic connection associated with money issues. You may be quite unaffected by the issue of financial security and at times spend freely and generously with friends and family members. Not so with Capricorn, who has a tendency to count the pennies and be more than moderately frugal. In a committed relationship this could take the form of a fight for control over the way money and resources are managed and spent. If you can deal with these issues and come to an initial understanding, it could relieve you of many ensuing financial dog-and-cat fights.

Though the eighth sector points to shared financial concerns, it is also a sexual sector and doesn't altogether discount the fact that Gemini may stimulate the Capricorn conservatism between the sheets. Capricorn will be entertained and relaxed by the playful nature of Gemini and to the extent that Capricorn will open up to your sexual approaches, this relationship could be the one redeeming factor in a long-term affair.

Capricorn will help to focus your many restless thoughts, Gemini, and clarify your direction if you allow them into your 'mind space'. You'll be surprised just how deep the Capricorn thought processes go. As Capricorn is ruled by the slow and steady Saturn, there is most definitely a deeper understanding that Capricorn may offer you, even if you both choose not to make this friendship a romantic one.

Most Capricorns won't vibrate compatibly with your nature, yet those born between 11 and 20 January should be considered, as they have similarities in their character, as do those Venus co-ruled Capricorns of 2 to 10 January. The most difficult group of Capricorns will be those born between 23 December and 1 January. Saturn's eighth rulership means their tight-fisted and sombre view of life is at odds with your free and easy nature.

Gemini + Aquarius   Air + Air = Wind

The karmic links between star signs of the same element are strong and usually karmically destined to bring fulfilment on many different levels. The Aquarian is a rebel, sometimes without a cause, and this brazen, freedom-loving attitude turns you on, Gemini. It reminds you of what you idealistically seek in life—variety, excitement and intellectual expansion. The planet Uranus ruling Aquarius brings with it much energy and this stimulates the restless spirit within you.

The strength in your sphere of intimacy will again rest upon your strong rapport as communicators. Both of you will spend pleasurable hours sharing your deepest thoughts, ideas and wild imaginations but, of course, there is a considerable difference between the intellectual expressions of Gemini and Aquarius. Gemini is happy to flit from one everyday topic to another in an incomplete fashion and can sometimes lack the depth and continuity that Aquarius prefers. The Aquarian is probably more focused and gives deeper consideration to the facts surrounding any given topic. It's not that Gemini can't keep up with this but Aquarius demands more focus from you, Gemini.

You feel a kinship with Aquarians and in particular those born between 31 January and 8 February. You will also be attracted to those born between 9 and 19 February, who offer you some interesting intimate moments. A more exciting and spontaneous friendship can be expected with Aquarians born between 21 and 31 January.

Gemini + Pisces   Air + Water = Rain

Gemini and Pisces are at right angles in the zodiac and therefore challenge each other in terms of their compatibility. Both of you are changeable in your views and experience of life. The ways you process your experience of love and the events surrounding your interaction with people are poles apart. Gemini, you have a preference for using your mind in your dealings with others.

Pisces doesn't necessarily shy away from social banter or other people's company, but tends to be receptive and communicative on a subtler level. If you wish to bond deeply with the Pisces mind and heart, you'll need to infuse your speech with an understanding of the deeper facets of nature. This is the way to draw them closer to you, as initially they may feel that you are far too cerebral for their liking. If you can express some sensitivity to the deeper and more receptive side of Pisces, you have the opportunity to prove to them that you are not simply all fluff and bubble. This will involve your taking moments to be silent and stop your chattering mind when you're spending time together. You will gain the respect of your Pisces friend and learn much more about what lies beneath your conscious and sometimes dispersed mind.

In coming together with a Pisces, those individuals born between 20 and 28 February are the most idealistic in a spiritual sense and will, if you give them a chance, stimulate your imagination beyond your dreams. The highly emotional and volatile Pisces born 1 to 10 March are probably a little harder to contain and connect with, due to the Moon in Cancer having sway over them. If it's passion you're after, and plenty of it, you'll do well with those born between 11 and 20 March, as Scorpio co-presides over their hearts. Lovemaking will be great with this lot, but expect some fierce intellectual competition from them as well.

Gemini + Aries   Air + Fire = Hot Air

Gemini undoubtedly stimulates Aries. You both interact quite explosively, with your Gemini element of air fanning the flames of the Aries fire. On both an intellectual and physical level, you and Aries enjoy first-rate friendship, conversation and inspiring times together, yet Aries could blow your Gemini mind as you live on your nerves and may not have the stamina and follow-through that Aries possesses.

Your romantic and sexual interaction will, without doubt, be a point of common interest, with your intellectual and clever mind continually inspiring Aries in ways you've never experienced before. You can spontaneously feel as though a river of ideas is flowing through you, due to this stimulating fire element of Aries doing its thing on you.

Between the sheets you'll both find ample room to explore that playful, childlike vigour you both possess and though you may not be destined for long-term marital ties, you can still have plenty of fun together. Aries seems to go headlong into everything, including love, romance and—you guessed it—lovemaking! You'll enjoy the brash raw heat of Aries, but also like the idea of playful discourse. There could be a need to spend time talking the hot-blooded Aries down a notch or two before consummating that love instinct within you.

Generally the combination of Gemini with Aries works well, yet look for those who are born between 11 and 20 April, as their co-ruler Jupiter has power over your marital and long-term affairs sector. Those born between 21 and 30 March will also become good friends, but those born between 31 March and 10 April may simply become good associates because of the communicational rapport you have with them.

Gemini + Taurus   Air + Earth = Dust

Though the planets Venus and Mercury, which rule Taurus and Gemini respectively, are friendly, there are some significant differences in your basic personality and motivation. For one thing,

Gemini, you prefer a faster and more rapid approach not only in your day-to-day life, but in your communication and mental style. Taurus prefers to delve more deeply and more methodically, solving a problem step by step or following a thread of an idea a stage at a time. You completely differ in that you jump from one idea to another with a high degree of curiosity and "scatter-gun" naivety. This doesn't mean Taurus isn't enamoured of your intellectual wit and humour—it's just that you need things to move at a faster and more hectic pace.

Both of you will have much to talk about and can spend many hours enjoying each other's company in wonderfully stimulating environments. You're both pleasure-seeking and like to do things that satisfy not just your intellectual but your emotional and cultural appetites, to which you are both drawn. On a point of intimacy, Taurus could be too slow-moving for your impatience, Gemini. If you are an evolved type, though, you may put the Taurean mental and conceptual abilities to good use and stimulate Taurus physically and sexually. If that is not the case you may find yourself leaving the Taurean bull high and dry in the bedroom. In some ways this combination is not bad, but your Mercurial character is a little too much for Taurus to handle.

By far the most beneficial combination offering you fulfilment is with those Taureans born between 30 April and 10 May. Their birthdays are strongly affected by Mercury, your own ruler. This means you'll feel that you both possess a lot of similar qualities, not the least of which is your playfulness. Those born between 21 and 29 April represent a moderately good combo with you, but they may feel as though you are intellectually condescending or patronising. They do have an intellectual calibre similar to your own. Just don't try to outshine them too often. With those born between 11 and 21 May you will find a steadying influence on your life. In short bursts you'll enjoy this equanimity, but may also start to feel a little smothered or weighed down in the process.

2006: THE
YEAR AHEAD

ROMANCE AND FRIENDSHIP

Your romance planet is Venus, which commences the year in retrogression in your eighth house of sexual encounters and self-transformation. There are ample opportunities for you this year to overcome any feelings of inadequacy you have been feeling in your relationships. This is pronounced as the year commences, but may ease up during February when you opt to back off from any impending confrontations with those you love. This may not be possible for just a while, however, as Venus moves to the opposition of Saturn in the early part of March, so most of the month will be a testing time for you – one in which you'll either sink or swim romantically. The months of April and May indicate a better time romantically when more favourable aspects shine on you and Venus gives you the chance to put any of those abrasive issues to bed. Venus also gives a wonderful social streak to your nature and your affairs around June, when it enters your sector of friendships. However, Mars, your friendship planet, causes some difficulties at this time and is seen to be in conflict with your romance planet. There may be disagreements over financial matters as the new Moon, Mars and Saturn are found to affect your monetary sector. October appears to be one of the more passionate months, in which the raw and vital energy of your physical and sexual nature will come to the fore. This is due to the proximity of Venus and Mars—and in your fifth romantic sector at that. Many Geminis who are single will find this period of 2006 very interesting indeed, with ample opportunity to meet new people and explore that side of their nature. If in a relationship and otherwise committed, this could prove to be another testing period as your existing partners may not fulfil you in matters of intimacy.

Venus enters the marriage sector in the latter part of November and remains there throughout December, hinting at opportunities for those interested in marriage to tie the knot at that time. The other fortunate aspect is from Jupiter, your

34

marriage planet. Jupiter, the Sun, Mars, Pluto and Mercury all combine in the very last month of 2006 to pave the way for some very exciting, if not challenging, long-term relationship cycles. There are periods in which you might be somewhat extreme in your relationships. Your communications can also be unwarranted, so you must curb your impulses. This is a year in which you have a chance to look at the deepest levels of meaning in your relationships. Remember that no one has to be right or wrong. You can both gain knowledge of the meaning of love and romance.

Quick-thinking and fast-paced Mercury is your ruling planet but also rules your domestic sphere and during 2006, the angular position of Mercury augers well generally for the affairs of your home. March, however, does see the retrogressive Mercury doing interesting things and this can affect your plans with family and relatives at this time. Decisions will not be easy and you may need to wait until the following month of April or even May till things are resolved. Mercury usually does the retrogressive movement three times a year, so in July as well as October expect more of the same in matters of family, residence or even business associated with real estate. You'll need to keep your wits about you when making important decisions. Most astrologers will usually advise you to take additional precautions if making purchases, signing documents or coming to critical agreements. September and October are also very important months in which much activity around your home and family will predominate. This could be simply the demands of those people upon you or even the re-connection or reunion with people you haven't seen for many years. September in particular will be a month in which you investigate and maybe even make some important long-term decisions about real estate, property and investment, as Mars, your profit planet, strongly influences the sign of Virgo, an earthy sign, in your residential sector.

Fundamental changes occur now and your need to break free from embedded life patterns becomes strong. You'll seek thrills and change rather than routine living. Relationships that have fallen into a cosy niche are not enough for you now. Even if you are not aware of the need to make changes, they will occur anyway. A chief relationship may break-up, form, or go through far-reaching changes. You may change jobs or become part of a different circle of friends and acquaintances. This is certainly a time to experiment with anything new, but be careful about what you throw out, because you can easily be gripped by a sense of urgency in the moment, and later lament your choice.

CAREER AND FINANCES

During 2006 your professional planets Uranus and Neptune exchange zodiac signs in a most extraordinary display of spiritual and innovative power for you, Gemini. How you handle these energies will determine not only the outcome for 2006, but for the next five or six years at least. For many Geminis this is a critical turning point. If you can now receive the inspirational vibrations of Neptune, as well as the dramatic and evolutionary promptings of Uranus, you'll be able to do something quite new and invigorating on your professional path to success. The year actually begins with a new Moon very near Uranus and Neptune and this further activates your desire for something novel, something different and unique. If you've been travelling along the same path in your work, 2006 will be a time for you to shake off your lethargy and finally make that break with your past.

As 2006 unfolds, you'll be able to move towards a larger view of your life. You'll seek new and broader horizons via travelling, studying, or reading about other cultures and by seeking out people who have a thoroughly novel approach to life. You'll be working on ways to imbibe these elements and relationships to give yourself a personal 'renovation' this year. This is surely a time to discard worn-out patterns of behaviour, to try new things and meet different people. It is likely to mark a time when your life direction and your significant goals and ambitions take on a new course, and even professional matters take a different path.

Uranus visiting your career sector tells you that unexpected results and benefits, right from the word go, will be a feature of your working environment throughout the whole of the year. Yet the new Moon in the early part, with the Sun also coming into contact with Uranus in March, will further accelerate these dramatic turning points for you. Neptune, which inspires you to do the unbelievable and to break free of your limiting material views of life, is still under the control of Saturn for some time yet. Though you will be bubbling over with ideas, it may be some time (probably August) until you can adequately formalise these ideas and make them a practical reality. In January, when the year kicks off, the Sun, the Moon and Venus activate the area of shared resources and the full Moon mid-month strongly focuses your attention on money that may be owed you and perhaps loose ends that weren't tied up in the previous year. It would be a good idea to tidy up these loose ends, especially with your creative impulses as strong as they are, so that you can move forward confidently, without too much financial baggage, so to speak. Though you may have some initial frustration in the first couple of months, the fine aspect of lucky Jupiter from your sixth working sector to your tenth professional sector will more than adequately compensate for any of the frustrations you may feel professionally in 2006. You'll be ready and raring to go and Mars also, from the early part of January, fully activates your luck by giving Jupiter a boost.

When the Sun enters Pisces in February, and then again in March and April, a huge wave of energy will wash over you and have you working hard. Again the months of July and then November are particularly strong as far as your work and profession are concerned. November is especially auspicious, as the combined influence of Sun and Jupiter bring you some welcome change in your work environment. Your friendly planet Venus transits your tenth house of career throughout the months of April and May and this could be a period of great popularity for you, when you may have the opportunity to rest on your laurels rather than having to do as much work as usual.

Fortunate conditions support your career this year. Whatever obstacles and challenges arise will fade away and your work for the most part will progress smoothly. This is a time of steady growth, combined with an enjoyable and harmonious atmosphere. You feel good about yourself and the direction of your life. Unusual or highly unforeseen events don't necessarily occur but the gradual change in tone and quality of your life brings about a much better situation for you. You may feel so comfortable, however, during this cycle that you do little to take full advantage of the opportunities that are available to you. Don't simply sit back and watch this influence pass you by!

KARMA AND LUCK

For the larger part of the year the lucky planet Jupiter is positive in your work sector and ensures many excellent opportunities for you throughout 2006. It is only in December that your truly magnificent luck is transferred to your relationships and even marital partners, if you are a married Gemini. This year is about creating opportunities and profiting from the work and service that you perform. Understanding those you work with in your professional arena will also enhance your luck quotient throughout this year.

Forging new relationships or even improving the current ones will be harder than you think, because Saturn is positioned in your third sector of communication and is in a challenging aspect to both Mars and Jupiter at the commencement of the year. You may have the vision but not the capacity initially to give the attention necessary to sort out personal differences with co-workers, for example. The karmic planet, the North Node, edges its way through your friendship sector until July. It will spend the rest of 2006 in your working and professional sector. This is indeed most lucky and indicates that some accolade will be achieved through the research or diligent work you conduct in your chosen profession. If you're a Gemini who has found it hard to find your niche in life and to act accordingly, then this is the commencement of a new eighteen-year cycle in your professional sector that could well mean you discover your true life path at this time. Your luck will centre on meaningful work and aligning your ego with your actions and professional aptitude. If you can do this and do it with confidence, then 2006 will be a year to remember as far as your professional achievements are concerned.

You must trust your instincts where it comes to the people offering you advice this year, Gemini. You may put certain people on a pedestal precisely when your judgment needs absolute clarity to make the decisions that are crucial in 2006. You could become disillusioned when you realise that the people you have admired are only human after all. It could be time to move on and re-align yourself with new friends, mentors and other advisers at this stage of your life.

There will be an important emphasis on your individual or private needs at this time. Hopefully you are associated with people who are trying to understand your situation and what you hope to achieve this year. You need plenty of support, especially from family members and peers. This is a marked period of spiritual growth and others may not always fully comprehend where you are exactly. It's up to you to help them understand. People evolve at different stages and degrees. You may find that even your closest allies are not moving ahead mentally or spiritually as fast as you would like. You must seriously consider the possibility that you've outgrown them this year!

Month By Month Predictions For 2006

JANUARY

Highlights of the Month

Your basic drive this month is shown to be of the behind-the-scenes type, as Mars activates much of your hidden talent. Though you'll achieve quite a bit, it will only be through careful and deliberate preparatory work. After the 12th, when the full Moon occurs in your finance sector, you'll reap some good monetary luck. The Sun and Moon both being in a finance sector this month shows that much of your attention will be in that area. The backward dance of Venus at the commencement of the month shows it's imperative you get all your facts and figures right with your professional and financial issues, as this will ensure a great start to your year. The strong new Moon on the 29th cautions you to be extremely diligent where any legal or technical matters are concerned. If you have put in the preparatory work earlier, things will resolve nicely at this time.

Be careful not to antagonise co-workers and superiors around the 5th as tensions are high around that time. In fact, this is generally so throughout this year, because Uranus is transiting your career sector the whole year long. The Sun entering Aquarius on the 20th, along with Mercury on the 22nd, indicates strong possibilities of either travel or interest in some educational pursuit.

Relationships could be under fire in the first few days, as Mars and Jupiter are in hard aspect. Fortunately, after the first week of January, your hot bed of potatoes may finally be cooked.

Romance and Friendship

From the first of the month you are inclined to invest your time and money into making your environment more attractive and comfy. You may also wish to boost your personal appearance in some way, such as getting a new hairstyle or purchasing clothing, cosmetics, and the like. Social gatherings are also very positive for you this month.

There are strong sexual connotations for the early part of the month as far as your relationships are concerned. Venus will move through that part of your horoscope that deals with the more hidden aspects of your relationships. It also appears that due to the difficult aspects between Saturn and Neptune, your communication could be somewhat stifled and if the deeper aspects of your relationship need to be discussed, not a lot of headway will be made in those first couple of weeks.

As Jupiter is your marriage planet and is slow-moving, things will not necessarily resolve as quickly as you'd like this year. This is particularly so because your partner may be preoccupied with other matters throughout the coming month and can't offer you the input or response you desire. There will, however, be some highlights and some exciting times around the 5th, 19th and 24th when the Moon transits your positive relationship areas. You'll need to use considerable imagination throughout this month and the combination of the Moon and Venus between the 1st and 3rd is critical if you're to satisfy your present emotional and physical needs.

As the month progresses you'll be less interested in small talk or insignificant babble, and you may find yourself avoiding neighbours or others in your close circle as a result. Also, you may have changed significantly over the past year or more, and you feel scratchy when people seem to be relating to the person you used to be, rather than who you are now.

Career and Finances

You'll certainly have to think big this month where your work and professional projects are concerned, especially around the 7th and 22nd when the Moon activates the strong Mars and Jupiter combination in your horoscope. Though you feel all fired up and ready to go, you have to diligently exercise control, make absolutely certain that your ideas have practical worth and that you definitely have the green light from those people who count. You may be acting impulsively and find later that what you had assumed had been given the thumbs up, actually had not.

Neptune, for most of the year your primary ruler of profession, receives the stifling influence of Saturn, which shows a conflict between your ideals and the practical implementing of those ideals. There can be some exciting encounters around the 19th when your career planet favourably influences you. There'll be some new encounters with people whose non-judgmental and understanding attitudes will stimulate your creative abilities and will help you along your work path. Some of these people you meet at this time may actually have some past karmic connections with you and so you will easily recognise them when you meet them.

Finances fluctuate somewhat this month, Gemini, and the first two weeks indicate a roller coaster ride. This will be punctuated by some fantastic financial gains or profiteering around the fifth, when the Moon enters the eleventh house in a favourable aspect to Pluto, hence showing your complete focus on monetary matters at that time.

Karma and Luck

Your lucky planet Venus is holding back from giving you what you desire this month and this may be the case for quite a few weeks as Venus re-enters the material sign of Capricorn. Sometimes the luck that we experience is delayed, or the actual pay-off is something we may have to wait for. This is not to say you won't have good fortune this month, but whatever benefits are achieved will be handed to you down the track by Lady Luck herself. Mostly this month will show that your personal charm is at a peak, yet your drive to take that to the world may be lacking. You can't hope to attract good fortune if you lock it away, Gemini. The other luck planet, Jupiter, continues its journey in your sixth house of service and therefore whatever good work or selfless activities are performed this month, especially around the 22nd and 23rd, will culminate in good karma for you. The presence of Jupiter in this area of health, and Venus influencing your Sun sign at the commencement of January, are protective of your physical being.

You may feel quite different in your social and personal life this month. You may be defiant and not want to comply with conservative or established role-playing or manners. This may prompt you to make changes in your overall viewpoints, as well as in your friendships. Old concepts could easily be discarded now as you yearn for a more distinctive and important course of action. You can remain unresponsive to the opinions of others. Furthermore, you may take an evasive position on emotional issues or anything that involves constraints or demands on your present lifestyle. Although your thinking is apt to be set on making progressive changes and reforms in your personal and social life, you must abstain from doing so in an unsettling or disordered fashion. That would put you at risk of being turned away from the ones you love.

Destiny Dates

High Times   5, 7, 12, 19, 20, 22, 23
....
Tough Karma   1, 3, 29
....

FEBRUARY

FEBRUARY

Highlights of the Month

Your relationships continue to dominate the affairs of February and this is particularly after the 3rd, when Venus, your planet of love and amusement, goes into direct motion again. This is activated even more powerfully around the 17th, when Mars enters your Sun sign and casts its fiery and passionate influence on your sector of relationships. It appears that February will be a critical month in which to bring your attention to the issue of relationships, love and even sexual matters. Try not to be too forceful throughout this month, as the extraordinary power of Mars may give others the impression you're trying to dominate them with your own brand of power and emotional manipulation.

Work matters are strongly focused after the 18th, when the Sun comes to the upper part of your horoscope and promises a new cycle in your work arena. Mercury too, around the 9th, prompts an important transition for you and indicates that the second and third weeks of February will indeed be weeks in which much communication will take place.

Romance and Friendship

You may have been reluctant to express your feelings before February got underway. However, after the 2nd, your need to convey your feelings will be quite pronounced and opportunities will arise with friends and lovers to do so. But be careful how you approach friends, because the combined influence of Moon and Mars around the 5th of the month can show that others may turn on you and change their minds about some previous agreements. Full Moon occurring on the 13th is highly beneficial for you and accelerates your communication and responses from those that count. You'll find it hard to stay away from the phone or the Internet during these few days and interesting conversations will ensue. An important letter or note may arrive and if you've been waiting for this, many things will become clear to you at that point.

Your domestic affairs are very powerfully activated on the 13th with unfinished family business reaching a peak around the 19th, when the Sun enters into a conflicting aspect with Mars. Earlier problems with friends and the advice you receive from those closest to you may be at odds and your impulsive nature may cause you to say and do things that you regret later. A friend has some gossip for you around this time as well. This could actually make you very restless and mentally active, if not even a bit nervous. Is it something that involves you? If not, you have absolutely nothing to fear, do you? It can feel like an electrical surge is pulsing through your body, though! In fact, you feel apprehensive about this new information because it challenges your innate idea of yourself. You can only make sense out of all of this if you don't operate from a base of fear. Don't be impulsive in meting out your vengeance at this time. It is far preferable to wait a day or two before stating your case. If you're travelling during this period as well, particularly when Venus enters a tough aspect with Uranus around the 20th to the 27th, avoid arguments and differences of opinion even if you know you're right.

Jupiter continues its tough transit in hard aspect to some of the planets, so long-term commitments or contracts should be avoided now. But the 28th is a new Moon and also coincides with the hard aspect of Mercury to Pluto, which means you have the opportunity to either rejuvenate your communications approach or find yourself being judged quite harshly by those you love most.

Career and Finances

Though your romantic cycle is not altogether favoured throughout the period of February, you can find your work becomes a fine outlet for you to move ahead in great strides. The month begins with your finance planet, the Moon, in the career sector. This is a wonderful omen, though changeable, to make you popular with the public and to achieve some good financial outcomes, especially around the 2nd and 3rd, as well as the 8th and 9th of the month. New contracts or at least very favourable discussions take place with employers or important people who can help you, around February when Mercury enters Pisces. The Sun also assists you in matters of work after the 18th when you can feel a great sense of power and self-worth.

Things may begin slowly as Mars continues its transit in your sector of private affairs and background activities. That changes dramatically after the 17th, when Mars enters your Sun sign and excites your personal initiative to an even greater extent. This is by far the best period to execute new plans or projects. Throughout the remainder of February, excellent aspects are formed between the outer planets Neptune and Uranus. These auger well for your creative dynamism and your quick-witted Gemini mind to find new ways to enhance your professional life. The period up to the 28th could be seen more as a preparatory period, but as soon as the new Moon occurs on that date, the green light is given to you to move forward with the exciting new plans you've decided to embark upon.

As the month winds down, especially after the 28th, working vigorously with a clear goal in mind assures you of success with the ideas you've been trying to convey to others. Some honour or recognition will be yours before the month is over and the benefits that follow are shown by continuing enquiries about your financial security during the movement of Venus in your eighth sector. Bank managers or other financial advisers can now join with you creatively to come up with some alternative methods of making money.

Karma and Luck
There are some great benefits due to the position of the Sun in your spiritual sector throughout the first two weeks of February.

Drawing upon your inner resources at this time will be a boon to all other departments of your life. You may have the opportunity to meet a mentor or to be introduced to someone whom you consider spiritually adept or evolved. This may happen or be facilitated through the advice or introduction of a friend. Though your initial reaction may be one of mistrust, it's not a bad idea to keep an open mind about these matters and to at least enter an "experimental" stage if you've not been exposed to them before. The spiritually lucky periods throughout the month are the 4th, 16th, and 25th, when these meetings are most likely to take place.

The obstruction of the lucky planet Jupiter, by Mars, fortunately softens after the 15th, when the service you've rendered others pays dividends. These may not always involve a financial remuneration, but rather a recognition of your talents. Reputation is always a precursor to financial and material benefits.

Destiny Dates

High Times   4, 8, 9, 13, 16, 17, 18, 19, 25

Tough Karma   2, 5, 28

MARCH

MARCH

Highlights of the Month

There is a great deal of activity in the heavens for you this month, Gemini. On the second, Mercury, your ruling planet, does a tail-spin, moves in reverse until the 20th and indicates that some of the plans you had earmarked for the month must be put on hold. This is particularly of note in matters of work and creative endeavours. Shortly after, on the 4th, Jupiter retrogresses also in a work-related arena and this may begin to impact strongly on the area in which you work. If changes or transfers have been on your mind, this could bring things to a head.

The excellent transit of Venus in the ninth house of journeys and good fortune accentuates the good possibilities for you from the fifth of the month onwards. Many Geminis will at last become clearer on what their long-term goals are, as this has quite an educational as well as spiritual significance. The overall plans you've made this month may see some unexpected changes and also necessary modifications, and this is also highlighted by the powerful combinations of Mars and Uranus that promise an eventful, exciting but somewhat erratic month.

This month also focuses much of your attention on family and relatives, and unexpected reunions with important family members are highlighted at this point.

Romance and Friendship

You may want to attempt new things as far as your romances are concerned. Aquarius is a progressive sign and being in your ninth sector of journeys, education and expansiveness, it's most likely that this cycle is one in which many new friendships and alliances can be formed. Though your domestic affairs are under re-evaluation this month due to Mercury's important movements, after the 13th you may be able to pursue some new romance that crosses your path, if you are unattached at this point. Actually, your ruling planet doesn't allow you to fully engage any of your friendships until the 26th, when it resumes its correct course. Both your working life and your domestic sphere are connected in some strange way, if only to keep you preoccupied to the exclusion of satisfying your social inclinations. Though this preoccupation hampers your ability to engage fully with others, some fine opportunities are found on the 5th and 6th when your excitable nature causes you to throw all cares to the wind and embark on an exciting new friendship. The advice to you at this point is to have a second and third thought before going too deeply in any new relationships that may emerge at this time.

The 15th and 20th are quite powerful dates for opening your heart to others and for others to feel your magnetic powers. For those Geminis currently in a relationship, however, some deeper work must take place, as the transformative Pluto continues to edge its way through your marital sector. Long-term committed relationships will, without a doubt, undergo incredible changes and when Pluto retrogresses on the 30th, a change of course in these relationships can certainly be expected. The new Moon on the 29th is also favourable for friendships and social get-togethers and several invitations may come your way, offering you some light relief from the heaviness of that Pluto energy.

Your mind may seem out of sorts at this juncture and you may even be perceived as having a chip on your shoulder whilst these planetary forces mould you. Someone may try to knock that chip off your shoulder, which could provoke you to an even more confrontational situation today. You're best to take some time alone and work through the internal conflicts that are bothering you.

Career and Finances

You have to pay special attention to the organisation of details this month in any business arena. The erratic and explosive energies of Mars and Uranus, along with the placement of Mercury in your career sector, at least until the 4th of the month, require delicate handling on your part. On the 1st you may find yourself banging your head against a brick wall trying to get your point across. This could take up a lot of your time and it needn't be so. The perfect antidote can be to step back, take a few deep breaths and think of the benefits you're bringing to the other party, especially if these people are employers or higher up. You can indeed achieve a lot this month and up till the 21st when the Sun enters Aries, a powerful surge of energy can either be successfully used or terribly misused by you. In this situation you're able to achieve recognition for what you have been doing professionally but you'll only gain the accolades you're after if you don't let others push your buttons and if you portray your honesty with a cool head.

Finances and monetary activities move into high gear after the 22nd and communication may take place about increasing your income or making some special arrangement with your employers over what you are paid. The full Moon of the 13th offers you a chance to quell the brash and fiery energies of Mars that are within your Sun sign now. The proposal you come into contact with at this point hints at the fact that remaining peaceful and cool under all trying circumstances is a clue to its imminent success. It is quite likely that there are individuals around you this month who are hard to please. So another clue to achieving success on your path is to be free of them, but this must be done in a way that doesn't increase your stress levels or grate on your social interaction.

The previous month or two afforded you the opportunity for the privacy you needed to muster your energies at this time. Don't blow it all for the sake of impulse and impatience. Good things come to those who wait. Wait until the seventh to discuss financial matters and even if reaching deeper to find greater significance in the work you're doing is a little difficult, you'll discover some understanding emerging.

Of course, the retrograde Jupiter on the 5th begs the karmic question of what your life work is and what the spiritual significance of your actions are at this point in time. You may need to concentrate deeply on these issues to come to an understanding. On the 25th the direct movement of your ruler Mercury resolves some of the issues and discussions surrounding these matters.

Karma and Luck

Pluto is concerned with tearing down the old to build up the new. The intensification of this primary principle comes into focus towards the end of March. Opportunities can only come to you as a result of letting go of those things in your life that are outdated, outmoded and a hindrance to further growth and prosperity. Your luck planet Jupiter also contributes along with Mercury this month to give you a sense of the need for reappraisal of the type of work you do, but more importantly of the way you express your needs when interacting with others.

Though the relationships have also been challenged to some extent, Venus' movement in your luck sector promises you good fortune and even financial opportunity through your social engagements and personal relationships this month. If an opportunity to travel is presented to you around the 24th or 25th, there may be a financial component involved that could be lucky.

Destiny Dates
High Times   5, 6, 13, 15, 20, 22, 26, 29

Tough Karma   4, 8, 9, 12

APRIL

APRIL

Highlights of the Month

There is a strong focus on popularity this month as Venus and Mercury, both highly favourable planets, accentuate your most prominent zodiac sector. This is the moment you've probably waited for. There's a chance to engage in entertainment, parties, and other exciting social interludes throughout the month of April. The tough aspects of Mars and Uranus are now clearing and even if some damage may have been caused in your relationships in the previous month, the soothing planetary rays of Mercury and Venus will help calm things down considerably. The hard taskmaster Saturn, who has been influencing your communications all through the first three months of the year, finally decides to move forward after the 5th.

Many Geminis will find their requests or enquiries into important changes or plans are coming to fruition. A strong drive for financial independence is evident on or about the 14th, when Mars enters your finance sector. Be careful not to spread yourself too thin and make sure that your heart is in the right place in terms of the way you earn, spend or share your financial resources at this time. On that matter you should be particularly careful up to April 20th, when the Sun exits your sector of friendships and social activities. You'll be lavishing much of that money on others and this is a mixed bag, both positive and negative, as far as those around you go. You don't want to appear to be buying friendship of coercing others with a generosity that may seem a little fake.

Romance and Friendship

The placement of Venus in its most powerful sign of Pisces occurs on the 6th and so the month of April is significant, heralding the commencement of a new and important phase in your romantic life. This is where your feelings of love and camaraderie can reach a positive peak and re-instil much confidence. You also begin the month with powerful and positive aspects between Venus and Mars that indicate a strong link between your social and sensual appetites this month. Those you are attracted to will find it much easier to overlook the shortcomings of your character just now and this gives you the distinct advantage in making the right impression.

The strong focus on romance is also accentuated by the full Moon of the 13th in your fifth sector of love affairs. As this falls within the same sign as the karmic planet this month, some of your past affairs or relationships may come to mind and if your karma is very strong, you may even find yourself in a chance meeting with a past lover or friend. This will no doubt result in some truly interesting exchanges, reminiscing and sharing aspects of your past with each other.

Throughout April you'll start to see the true face of the people around you and those who were once friends are now exhibiting their human frailties. How are you going to deal with this? Again, you either accept people with their blemishes and all, or you move on. Difficulties occur when you have to meet, greet and work with these people on a daily basis. That requires diplomatic abilities to juggle the many personalities around you.

On the domestic front things start to move ahead quite strongly and Mercury shows you're prepared to make some concessions by accepting an invitation to be part of the family dynamic. Respectfully declining an offer at this time might be tantamount to an insult on your part. Be gracious and accept what is given as this will cement your relationships with those people who, in the long run, really are key players in your life. The full Moon of the 13th and days on either side may bring to the fore an issue surrounding a younger person in your life and this needs to be dealt with. There could be a component of health or financial waste associated with this person and your timely advice will be of much use to certain family members.

Career and Finances

Even if you have to deal with coercive or manipulative people now, strive to cooperate with them for the benefit of third parties. Otherwise, you might have to deal with angry, jealous or spiteful behaviour directed your way. You must also be aware that your own anger may be lying just below the surface, and it could take only a minor incident or disagreement at work to trigger your temper. Concentrate on health issues, too. You can use your popularity to great advantage now —also to deal with these very issues.

The incredibly fortunate placement of Mercury and Venus assure you of success throughout April 2006. On the first and second be careful of absentmindedness that no amount of popularity can undo. You may leave behind important papers or could simply overlook an engagement or important appointment that may have uncomfortable repercussions for you. Meetings could develop strongly throughout the month and around the 15th and 16th, when the Moon enters the same sign as Pluto, bring results that can help you break out of the temporary rut you may find yourself in. You can put on your best character around this time and mesmerise others with your dramatic flair and keen insight. If you're in business and wanting to close a deal, the 16th, 17th, 23rd and 24th are perfect days to do so.

Although finances continue to be a key focus, the Mars placement in Cancer may cause you to be overly emotional and thereby somewhat sloppy in the way you tie up your financial loose ends this month. You need to balance your fiscal attitude and create some definition around those impractical hare-brained projects you may be working on. Don't lose focus or be distracted from a clear-cut plan at this point. The 4th and 5th as well as the 25th are powerful days to get your books in order. On the 23rd don't mix business with pleasure and try to curb your scepticism about a younger professional who hits the scene, albeit temporarily.

Karma and Luck

The physical and sensual expressions of your nature will be some of the more important luck generators this month, Gemini. With the critical transit of Venus in its best position, it will not be that hard for you to exude the right sort of energy in attracting luck, both materially and emotionally. You'll feel a distinct uplifting in your luck quotient around the 6th and also socially when Mercury enters Aries around the 16th. The entry of the Sun into Taurus could slow things down after the 20th and this is again a period of approximately a month for you to quietly reflect on the spiritual side of your nature and how that impacts upon your overall good luck and fortune in life.

Fortunate circumstances assist you in your life. Exciting changes in your career path present themselves to you at this point. You may be nervous about the ground shifting beneath your feet—don't! It's best to wait for these opportunities shortly. If the changes appear to be coming from unexpected quarters, don't immediately assume defence mode. Sometimes it is life bringing you the needed changes for further improved growth.

Destiny Dates

High Times   4, 5, 6, 13, 16, 17, 23, 24, 25

Tough Karma   1, 10, 12, 18, 20

MAY

MAY

Highlights of the Month

The full Moon on the 13th brings new opportunities in work and also a renewed vigour to improve matters of health and diet in particular. Your exercise regimen will continue to be an important element of your life but this is probably due more to the influence of someone having a quiet word in your ear at this time. You probably realise that your ideal or optimal look or physical feelings are not in keeping with the reality of your physical self. The full Moon brings these issues to the fore.

The Sun remains in the quiet sector of Taurus for you until the 20th, when a slightly introverted period or time-out segment of your life finishes and you'll move full steam ahead. Moreover, Venus is now moving in your social sector. All this means that a dynamic social cycle is forecast at least for the remaining two weeks of the month. Though the invitations are proffered after the 3rd you'll still need time alone to do the serious work on your thoughts and plans. Mercury also enters Taurus on the 5th, so you'll be doing some serious soul-searching and also wondering perhaps how you can benefit others in the larger scheme of things at this point in your life. The thoughts do turn to more spiritual and humanitarian matters.

Financial issues can come to an abrupt head around the 8th, with plenty of Martian energy to help stimulate you into action at this time. A whole new process commences in your financial life, but try not to be too emotional about the way you see things as there's a tendency to want to push forward quickly as soon as the idea comes to mind. This is an important challenge for you as you are dealing with the more altruistic thoughts of how to help others whilst the more practical side of your nature is saying to save money, be more frugal. These two desires are in conflict with each other. Around the 12th Mercury will enter into the company of the Sun and this will help steer you to a much clearer view of how to reconcile these issues. Somehow you'll be offered an intuitive breakthrough that will put a smile on your face.

Between the 10th and the 12th domestic matters call for some urgent intervention on your part. A miscommunication could throw a different complexion on matters this month and this has occurred just at a point when you were starting to get your thoughts in order. You'll need to express yourself clearly and also listen carefully to the message between the lines when others try to be a little evasive perhaps or even deceptive. Don't be afraid to ask the hard questions of those whom you feel are trying to put pressure on you.

The new Moon of the 27th begins to cement a lot of your ideas and brings many of the threads of your thinking together in a positive way at this time.

Romance and Friendship

Throughout the month of May Venus moves swiftly through your career sector up into your romance sector on the 3rd and then into your spiritual sector on the 29th. This shows that your love cycle oscillates between your work and social obligations and finally moves into a more karmic and soul-searching period, which continues into the following month. You'll probably be burning the candle at both ends as the month starts and you possibly know you should be exercising more self control, have more focused intentions and frugality where your social and love life are concerned, but you'll more than likely throw all caution to the wind. Again on the 7th you may find yourself having to shake yourself and give yourself a reality check over your misguided perceptions of another person. You have a strong desire to make your romantic dreams a reality, but the earlier part of the month could dash your hopes. It's not until Venus forms a favourable aspect with Saturn around the eighth that you can indeed experience a settling of your emotions and a more realistic view of the likelihood of your relationships working. This is more pronounced if you're single, but for those married Geminis this too can be an important development in relationships: a steadying of the feelings and a sense of obligation may return things to an even keel.

Other dates to watch out for, in which your love affairs and/or creative endeavours are likely to be accentuated, are the 14th, 15th and 20th. Some interesting and unexpected avenues open up to you and this can herald the beginning of a new phase of love in your life, especially if you're unattached. Your popularity is particularly notable after the 21st, when the Sun enters the sign of Gemini. Don't try hard to be popular, as the Sun naturally enhances your magnetic appeal and people will want to be in your company. You're advised to put in less effort in the first part of May until the solar energy comes your way. Try to exercise some discrimination, however, around the 23rd, when Venus enters into difficult aspect with Mars. Your desire for sensual and even sexual escapades could land you in trouble. Venus transits to the quieter and more spiritual sector of your horoscope on the 29th, when your romantic energies are quelled somewhat.

The health of loved ones comes into focus around the 23rd. Try to be available to give timely advice and maybe even some financial assistance; they may be worrying about some governmental or domestic issues.

Career and Finances

With Mercury moving into your personal sector after the 19th and the full Moon on the 13th, the five-or-six-day period surrounding these phenomena is a strong testimony that your self-image is about to change with respect to the way you do business and indeed the way you approach your work. The position of Mercury in its own sign of Gemini is excellent in giving you a renewed sense of self and wholly new perspective on money in terms of who you are, rather than what you have. Mercury gets energised so your intellectual energies will be very stimulated throughout

63

this month, particularly when Mercury comes to Gemini. You may have some fresh ideas about changing your presentation and the way people see you in business and this could happen around the 3rd of the month. Some time around the 8th you may need to reconfirm the commitment you have to expressing who you really are, rather than presenting yourself the way others expect you to be.

Once you get your self-image sorted out you can expect an extremely busy month, when it may appear the wolves are at your door staking out their pound of flesh. Around the 4th and 5th, be careful not to promise more than you can deliver in terms of your workload. There may be a couple of difficult days as far as your professional life is concerned. Your professional planets of Mars and Jupiter begin the month in a friendly aspect so you're more than likely to have the energy and the drive required to accomplish what you set your mind to. That's quite likely too because of your renewed commitment to improving your health and making the most of the personal energies at your disposal. There's no time to be frivolously eroding your days with useless activities and this is seen to dominate your affairs professionally and financially throughout the month of May. On the 2nd, the 11th and also on the full Moon of the 13th, as well as the 20th and 22nd, some strong professional highlights are to be expected. People who would like you to think they have their act together may not. When the deadlines arrive, they may not be quite as prepared as you would like them to be. Some of their inadequacies may be projected upon you and unless you're prepared for these moments of abrupt turnaround, you could find yourself having to pick up the pieces on their behalf.

For Geminis, either working independently or as agents, the period of the 2nd to the 13th is an excellent time for picking up new business or anticipating some additional sources of income through referrals.

Karma and Luck

Developing your self-image is the strongest element of luck for you throughout May. With the energising of your Sun sign by Mercury and the favourable connections between Mars and Jupiter, your luck will depend strongly on the way you present yourself physically and in terms of your communication style. You may need to consider your attire, fashion and other objects that make a strong statement to the world about who you are and how you're prepared to deal with others in relationships—whether socially or professionally. When Mars enters favourable aspect with Jupiter around May, if you've polished your self-image and presentation finely enough, some excellent remuneration may float your way. Don't forget, too, that the colour green has a strong and energising effect on the sign of Gemini and so you may wish to include this in your strategy to enhance your luck and fortune this month.

Destiny Dates

High Times   2, 3, 5, 13, 14, 15, 20, 22, 26, 29

Tough Karma   4, 7, 10, 11, 12, 23

JUNE

JUNE

Highlights of the Month

Travel will certainly be strong on your agenda this month as Mars moves to your third sector of journeys and communication. This occurs on the 3rd and also brings with it a lot of social activity in its wake. You'll be experiencing a strong shift from the financial and work drive to the area of exploration and daredevilishness. This may be necessary as the month commences with the Moon hemmed in between Mars and Saturn, which has a harrowing aspect over the more financial and material elements of your life. You may need to simply get away and have time to let some of these matters or nature take its own course.

You must not let any of your emotional frustrations build up this month as it's evident from the intensifying relationship between the Sun and Pluto that your communications could become extremely intense, if not manipulative, by the 16th, when these energies are at their peak. Around the same time, after the 19th, Uranus, the planet which is strongly associated with your work and profession throughout 2006, does its retrograde dance and causes a rethink about your professional direction. There are now elements of mistrust both in your work and your relationships of a personal nature. Apart from the physical rest that some travels may afford you, they give you a chance to reappraise the value of your relationships. For many Geminis these could appear to be dominated by their partners or friends, so they need to summon their own power to reclaim a sense of equality in those relationships.

Romance and Friendship

The transit of Mercury into Cancer on or about the 3rd activates your continued desire to perfect your financial dealings. But that won't dominate your thinking for too long as Mars and its association with Saturn simultaneously produce frustration both with these financial issues of yours and the people who surround them. You're at a crossroads, and on the 5th, the tight associa-tion of these two planets means you can either learn from the relationships you're in or you may have to let them go. Tightening these relationships and the way you feel about significant other lovers or romantic partners is strongly focused around the 4th, when your love planet forms a right angle with Saturn.

Throughout the early part of the month you'll be given to dis-cussing the more private side of your needs and your interactions could become quite intense and revealing, as might the other parties' revelations. You're not going to be satisfied with the simple answers that are given now in any of your relationships and therefore any of the previous obstructions will be broken down this month. You have an opportunity throughout June to transform any of your relationship negativities into a new opti-mistic outlook. Meeting with people who share common ideals or purposes will be very successful now. You may have meetings which occasionally arise out of the most unforeseen encounters. You could meet someone shortly who changes your world view or presents you with the tools and opportunity to make your mark in some significant area of life. Be alert to these current pos-sibilities. Take full advantage of them in the first few days of the month, as Venus will move into a quieter mode within the first week of June.

Around the 14th you can feel amorous, as the full Moon is conducive to love and even marriage proposals. The 20th and 23rd also indicate strong passions and love opportunities for Gemini. Turn those high-strung tensions into an occasion of re-ciprocal giving by planning a special night out with the one you love. Blind dates are also given the green light as you could meet Mr or Ms Right around this time.

Beauty may appear to you in a different form during the month of June. Your sense of beauty and communications amalgamate to make great first impressions now. You can also combine your social life and these surprising love vibrations with travel opportunities, particularly after the 3rd. Hot, sub-tropical travel resorts would be ideal to enjoy yourself and explore romance. If you've had to let go of a lover or friend, the period of the 10th to 15th brings up some ghosts of the past or skeletons in the closet. You must occupy yourself now with positive thoughts and realise that out of the old the new is born. Social responsibilities may also tire you considerably.

Step around the 15th or 16th and dance to a different tune. Now you can creatively go beyond the limits of who you thought you were. This can be attractive to others. The 19th is also a great day to break loose from "the square". Good news warms your heart around the 20th and being with relatives gives you a needed insight or two.

Career and Finances

As June gets under way communications could stall and it may be due to an oversight on your part. Diligently look over your notes or diaries to check the timing and commitments given by both sides before you come out with all your guns blazing. The new and full Moon is pointing the way financially this month. Antiques are also a strong bet for investing your money and time and will prove a source of good fortune. You needn't spend much, however, and artefacts such as feng shui, Buddhas or other good luck charms of an antique nature will appeal to you, bringing luck and fortune your way.

Hone your skills around the 11th, as a business meeting possesses all the hallmarks of future prosperity. If you can control your mind and temper under this adverse planetary aspect, the future results will be numerous.

From the 12th to the 20th you can also experience an increase of luck due to the Sun returning to Gemini. Be realistic, though, as you'll be thinking big and you could be overlooking

69

some of the more concrete matters of your existence. There's no doubt your boldness of spirit and sense of adventure is on the increase and it's best to act a little more prudently, especially if you are undertaking any new business or commitment.

As the month concludes, you may be feeling inadequate or comparing yourself to those more privileged and this is definitely a formula for disappointment and aggravation. You may be dreaming of "what could have been" or "what if". The fact is that you are what you are and this month calls for a mindset of contentment and appreciation if you are to avoid spiralling into the self-defeating sentiment of "not enough".

Karma and Luck
At the outset of the month, due to your festive, partying mood, you will just want to play and share good times with your friends. Parties and other invitations to social events will make you feel fortunate and popular. This will be occupying your mind. Also, at this time it is hard for you to say no to food, drink, or extravagances in any form. You're therefore likely to regret your actions later if you don't curtail your impulses to overindulge, overspend, and enjoy too much of a good thing.

Towards the middle of June, due to your indiscretions, you aren't likely to be very gregarious or sociable, and you may feel that you cannot be openly affectionate with someone you care about. You may have romantic yearnings for someone who is unavailable to you, and great discretion regarding this relationship may be called for. On the other hand, this can be a spiritually revealing time. You could be called upon to give to or care for others without getting much personal enjoyment or pleasure for yourself, except through serving them in an unselfish way.

Destiny Dates
High Times   3, 11, 14, 18, 19, 20, 23
....
Tough Karma   5, 10, 12, 15
....

JULY

Highlights of the Month

Venus ensures this is one of your better months in 2006, Gemini. Attraction, beauty, art, music and other refined or cultural activities set the tone for this month. Interesting and thoroughly stimulating activities of the previous month continue. The positive forward movement of Jupiter promises that work, health and other matters are resolved sufficiently enough to allow you to fully enjoy the benefits of Venus. Continue, however, to exercise restraint and discernment.

Another important highlight this month is the retrogression of Mercury between the 5th and the 30th and the full Moon of the 11th focuses this energy. Finances may temporarily intrude on your space again, and sorting out money with partners requires constructive decisions on your part. Venus moves to Cancer on the 19th and focuses a tremendous amount of energy on your domestic sphere. Work around the home seems to centre on tasks that have been postponed and this will feature heavily around this time. Mars moving to Virgo on the 22nd is quite constructive inasmuch as your money and your home affairs are concerned and the two come together at this point. That will be considerably focused around the 28th, when important yet heavy communications require your compassionate but stern and consistent responses to others. This will be considerably tiring as it also involves the conjunction of Sun with Saturn. Your karmic planet is in Virgo just now and many past family issues will resurface and will need to be addressed this time. Your mother and matters associated with her or other female members of your family will demand your attention in a big way.

Romance and Friendship

Excessive responses due to overconfidence need to be monitored this month. Though you have the right blend of magnetism and timing to lure people your way, you could overextend yourself and also burn some bridges along the way. Be moderate in your response even if others appear completely enamoured of you.

The more favourable romantic dates in July are the 2nd, 10th, 15th, 27th and 30th when Venus creates lucky encounters for you. You prefer the first part of the month to include those you are familiar with rather than venturing into uncharted romantic territory. Cementing your love ties in the first week of July is a good idea. Expect the unexpected on the 6th when an already hectic agenda is aggravated by even more unrealistic social expectations. What do your friends think you are—superhuman?

Beautiful, spiritual and soul mate connections are likely around the 10th, when Neptune brings you glimpses of "love possibilities". Your emotional dreams could materialise at that time. Difficult romantic dates are to be watched for on the 14th, 16th and 22nd. Don't expect too much from that date or social engagement. It could leave you feeling somewhat flat.

Your domestic life is given a boost after the 22nd. Due to the presence of Mars, unfinished renovations, building, gardening and other odd jobs will begin to see completion stage. It's a great time to get your hands dirty and clean up those unsightly areas around your home. Work on vehicles and other machinery, computers etc. may also require your attention during this cycle.

Because Mercury is retrograde it is inadvisable to make important decisions regarding your domestic life. Changing your residence on a whim is discouraged and you'll find that after the 29th your common sense will again prevail and have you asking, "what was I thinking?" The 1st and 28th are also very strong dates for domestic activities. Some in-house entertainment is not a bad idea on those dates.

Career and Finances

The Sun enters Leo on the 22nd and with the new Moon of the 25th, important work matters come to light but not without some high-strung tensions on the 1st and 2nd. On the 6th as well, your nerves get the better of you and with Jupiter's forward movement on the same day, deadlines change without your knowledge, leaving you "holding the baby" at work so to speak. Until the 22nd, when Mars is transiting Virgo, your anxieties will be exaggerated and business dealings become nebulous. Legal matters, if on your agenda, can be awfully confusing and enemies or adversaries adopt underhanded tactics to usurp you.

Around the 10th you'll be confronted with more paperwork, contracts or agreements with third parties demanding your signature. This isn't to cherish your autograph, by the way—don't be pressured into saying "yes" when your heart says "no".

The full Moon of the 11th moves finances along but don't expect any easy gains or windfalls. This is more a matter of financial planning and clarity. On the 12th and 13th, your mind oscillates between moments of brilliant idealism and confusion. In fact all legal matters and other paperwork are best left until after the 30th of the month.

The 14th is an important day professionally and as the week finishes your brilliant flashes of inspiration save the day. A lull in the team's creative efforts sees a light at the end of the tunnel, thanks to you. By all means, speak your mind and let others experience your progressive side today. Venus moves to Cancer on the 19th and Mars to Virgo on the 22nd, with the Sun in Leo on the same day. This is not a particularly good combination for your financial prudence. Spend on those necessary gifts if you must, but remember, it's the thought that counts, not so much the amount you spend.

By the 27th any underhanded manoeuvres of your work associates may be uncovered and dealt with. Hired hands, servants or other assistants will also show their other side. How will you deal with this? Decisions, decisions!

Karma and Luck

On the 7th the luck planet Jupiter moves full-steam ahead, with the 15th and 24th bringing you some gifts, accolades or even your own pat on the back for what you consider a job well done. Until the 19th your personal magnetism is what continues to carry you along and you'll wonder how you got through some of the difficulties of July, when all is said and done. The answer? Sheer charm.

Venus hints at a special connection with foreigners and other cultures as well as spiritual disciplines that may not have appealed to you previously. Due to the concurrent movement of the karmic planet, the North Node, from your friendship sector to your professional sector, a new phase of lucky friendships commences, as old worn-out ones are discarded. Oh well, what goes around comes around. Lucky connections now begin in your work sphere as well. More about this in August.

Destiny Dates

High Times   1, 2, 12, 15, 19, 24, 28, 30

Tough Karma   5, 10, 11, 22, 27

AUGUST

AUGUST

Highlights of the Month

For the first time in 18 years, the primary karmic planet, the North Node, edges its way through your career arena. For many Geminis the time is now right for the tying up of professional karma, work commitments and other vocational issues. If the work you've been doing (or has it been doing you?) has lost its flavour, you can now feel the strong planetary vibrations encouraging you to do what you really love. Unfortunately, new work patterns, job opportunities and other life path changes may be far too radical for you to take up immediately. Though your heart knows what it wants and what is probably best, your head may be doing battle with it.

As Mars is moving away from Saturn now, less frustration generally will be felt in your relationships and you'll have loads of dynamic energy freed up to explore other avenues of mental and physical pleasure and fulfilment. Both Mercury and Venus, around the 10th and 12th respectively, enter Leo and this is a wonderfully liberating mental vibration. Yet the hard energies of Mars indicate physical risks, high-end sports and other physically demanding activities involving risk that ought to be minimised.

The full Moon of the 9th is an important one and coincides with the movement of Mercury and Venus in your communication sector. This highlights your need for fresh spiritual undertakings, study that involves friends and lovers and possibly a complete revamp of your life view overall. Sun enters Virgo on the 23rd and Mercury does the same on the 27th. Home life takes the limelight again as the month ends.

Romance and Friendship

Mars, South Node and the Sun will all drag you into domestic demands the final week of August, in spite of yourself. There's no escaping the odd confrontation or two as these fiery planets all combine now. The 22nd and 23rd are hot spots to be on the look-out for. These issues commence when your family planet Mercury enters Leo around the tenth. Relatives are simply airing their grievances and you shouldn't overreact under these transits. As Venus also enters Leo on the 12th much of what is to follow can be quelled by recollecting your previously successful charm phase, which can win others over, including family members.

The Moon in your romance sector is again great for love and affairs of the heart but when Venus associates with Saturn on the 26th, you must do your utmost to pursue the ideal of duty and obligation to your commitments, rather than follow your more carnal appetites. You could feel as though your partner or even someone new on the block is either demanding too much of your love or is not expressing their true feelings. On the 27th either you or someone you're involved with may want to overdrama-tise the situation, which could make things worse than they are. Maintain equanimity in the last week of August. Finally, on the romantic front, the volatile Mars/Pluto aspect on the 29th, there is a potential world war if you let it be. The key word this month may well be "composure".

Social engagements fare well, especially around the 4th, 9th (full Moon) 14th and 17th. Around the ninth, someone whispers a surprising secret in your ear, but the repercussions of this information may not be fully felt until the 20th, when you're con-fronted with some revelation of the "real" story. Keep your mouth shut and eyes and ears open.

Career and Finances

A powerful professional phase begins for Gemini in August 2006. The karmic North Node brings its energies to your work and kar-ma sector. For the first time in 18 years, the complete reappraisal of your professional direction is upon you. Even if you choose to turn a blind eye to the inevitability of this pattern you will at some time in the coming 18 months be forced to make some significant decisions in this regard. If you've been stuck in a rut doing work that is not heartfelt or creative, now is the time to step onto your true life path.

Saturn continues to challenge your progressive thinking on these matters as Uranus demands change. Out with the old, in with the new. In some cases redundancies and payout packages will be offered but if fear dominates your decisions now, the outcome will be less than favourable in the long term.

Your authority is challenged around the second, when employers or those who know better are asking you to prove your skills. A complete rest may be the answer as the Sun joins Saturn around the seventh. If you have a sick day or two up your sleeve, take them.

There is an improvement in your confidence and a job opportunity presents itself around the ninth. If your sense of adventure and love of the unknown are sufficiently developed, you'll jump at the chance to resonate with the new and exciting karmic possibilities in your vocation.

Missed calls, abusive letters, miscommunications, problems with computers, software and in general any work-related equipment may exasperate you on the 18th. Much of your valuable time may be eroded over the period from the 18th to the 20th trying to sort out these issues. The entry of the Sun into your domestic sector on the 23rd is opposing your work and signifies a need to execute your duties in a more cloistered environment. Stepping away from the crowd and working at your own pace is advisable. Be sure to dress in sync with what the occasion requires around the 23rd and also spend your money on items that are appropriate to the people concerned. Chins could be wagging behind your back if you dress or spend inappropriately.

As the Moon hints at speculation this month, investigate stocks and other financial strategies on the 13th, 23rd and 28th.

The new Moon of the 23rd points to your inner self as a source of renewed power now as well.

Karma and Luck

The professional arena of your life continues to dominate your activities. You can either impress or push away the positive karma that employers offer you this month. Work to draw the best out of others who can help your cause.

Some hidden wealth, either tied up with government departments, banks, insurance or stocks and annuities may come to light. Investigate your old or supposedly closed bank accounts to ferret out any lost money. Other misplaced objects come to light, too, or suddenly appear when you least expect it.

Due to the power of your domestic cycle, cleaning out nooks and crannies is revealing, especially on the 22nd and 23rd around the new Moon. Meditation and dreams are revealing around the 9th to the 15th.

Destiny Dates

High Times	4, 9, 10, 12, 14, 17, 23, 28
Tough Karma	11, 18, 22, 26, 27

SEPTEMBER

SEPTEMBER

Highlights of the Month

Family reunions, resolving issues of the past, making plans for a more stable domestic environment and generally strong family ties are the prominent features of September 2006 for Gemini. These are pronounced especially in the first week of the month. Relationships later take precedence, especially on the 6th, 7th, 12th and 23rd, when four planets stimulate your romantic appetites. Pluto's forward movement on the 4th dominates the emotional life of your partners and lovers. You'll know something important is happening emotionally to them but you can't quite put your finger on it. You'll need plenty of intuition and diplomacy in this life department during September. The full Moon occurs in your professional sector near the karmic planet, the North Node. Those important decisions in work may now have the practical follow-through you'd hoped for. Employers may treat you to sweet words and kind gestures, and your responses will prove to be a financial boon to you.

It's an enthusiastic month and can be one where you feel all fired up again. Those new doors are opening up for you, especially in professional areas. Unconventional ways of doing things will help you surge ahead, while good fortune and even wins in lottery, gambling and other games of chance are given the thumbs up by Uranus and Jupiter, who are in good aspect this month.

If you begin new things in September they will bring you great satisfaction but you mustn't rest on your laurels. Some Geminis will prefer in spite of this to remain more mellow and contented with things as they are, but that won't be the case generally.

Tensions in romantic matters certainly ease this month. Both you and your partner will now be emphasising the positive rather than the negative in your relationship. Even if the temptation to venture beyond your current relationship is there, you'll probably feel satisfied enough to stay where you are, realising that the grass isn't necessarily greener on the other side.

Romance and Friendship

For the most part this month will bring you satisfaction in your love and romantic affairs. Because your domestic sector is still strongly active you feel contented in your own space and will more than likely choose to do some entertaining on your home turf during this period. Some sizzling moments of passion around the 3rd defuse any over-serious discussions of the 4th, when Pluto moves direct. The 5th also sparks your intuition with some zesty moments, and unattached Geminis should trust their gut feelings when that pair of attractive eyes meets theirs. You may want anything but a practical stay-at-home night on this occasion, even though domestic vibes set the general trend.

Venus enters Virgo on the 6th and Mercury in weird aspect to Neptune dampens your love meter temporarily. Don't try too hard to win your lover's approval today. Around the 10th Moon, Venus and Uranus combine and urge you to socialise. You'll want to share your comfortable space with others and pamper them with love, affection, and sumptuous food, as well as some words of wisdom.

Around the 5th, 9th and 18th the health of a loved one may cause concerns. Both their lifestyle and dietary habits need an overhaul and you'll be called upon to make sense of their attitudes to their physical wellbeing. Visits to hospitals, sanatoriums and community groups or aid organisations may also be likely at this time.

On the 2nd, 10th, 22nd and 23rd favourable planetary omens abound and engagements, weddings and other celebratory functions call for your attendance. Discussions about your own long-term marital prospects also surface and this occurs on the 2nd and 22nd, around the new Moon.

With the Sun's entry into the fifth sector your daredevil spirit and sporting prowess is activated. Social activities will centre on sporting events and other outdoor fun. The 23rd and 24th are physically and socially very empowering.

Career and Finances

Under no circumstances. sweep your work backlog under the rug. The period after the 23rd could mean there is no going back and asking for second chances to meet your deadlines. Prior to this date, however, several opportunities come your way. Perhaps you'll start to get used to the karmic blessings of the North Node in your professional sector. If you have any problems in the early part of September, it will be sifting the wheat from the chaff. Which opportunities are genuine and will assist you in the long term and which are to be discarded? These are the important questions just now.

The full Moon on the 7th presents you with a new job opportunity, but those closer to home threaten to dampen your hopes with doubts about the validity of this offer or your capacity to handle it. Listen to them before you make your decision as there may well be some truth to their advice.

Anything can happen now with Uranus still hovering in your work sector. Important and positive dates that have a bearing on work include the 3rd, 6th, 7th, 19th, 23rd and 25th. The 3rd requires your input at a conference or study seminar. You'll have to brush up on your skills in presenting your ideas to others as well as the work itself. On the 6th control your impatience, for work or construction in your work arena affects your nerves and your temper. You have to let go of what you have no control over. The 7th is karmically illuminating and generous. You can land that coveted job or position. Work on your resume and make sure your facts, dates and figures are up to scratch. Don't forget to enter the work raffle or lottery as your luck is strong now.

Your vocational energy could run dry by the 23rd, when the Sun moves to Libra. Keep a little in reserve and get extra sleep in the last week of the month.

Finances are excellent on the whole as the Moon, your money ruler, is in Sagittarius when the month commences. You could be working on a new get-rich-quick scheme this month, but you realise that what comes easily can disappear just as quickly. The 16th, 19th and 30th are all financially focused days and positive for your acquisition.

Karma and Luck

Lucky Jupiter maintains its beneficial stance due to Uranus. Opportunities to win and acquire material goods and money are very likely this month, so you won't have to push too hard to reap those positive karmic fruits.

On the 18th go the extra mile and travel with a friend, even if it seems hard work. The results will surprise and uplift you. During that time together, sharing your thoughts and feelings will create an even stronger bond between you. You may not realise it but when you open up to others they want to help you and this is the first stage of success and fortune.

Work prospects bring new and unexpected financial horizons into view. Some forgotten letter or proposal you presented a while ago suddenly returns with a positive answer and optimistic outcome.

Destiny Dates

High Times   2, 6, 7, 10, 12, 22, 25, 30
....
Tough Karma   3, 4, 5, 9, 18, 23
....

OCTOBER

OCTOBER

Highlights of the Month

As Mercury enters Scorpio on the 2nd into your service sector, you'll be looking at new ways to accomplish your goals. Techniques and systems you've been utilising to plan your day and get things done now seem outmoded or inefficient to you. As your personal planet, the association of Mercury with Jupiter for the first time in nearly a year is also very promising. You'll feel as though you've struck gold when solving some of life's problems, and their solutions will come to you, as if by divine dispensation. The peak of this effect is on the 22nd.

As a result of your mind being cleared of some routine glitches, the full Moon on the 7th in your social sector finds you looking for company yet again. Your friendship planet Mars in Libra grabs your attention as those you considered friends may reveal deeper romantic motivations. Surprising, but nevertheless very flattering.

These important developments relating to your bodily health are accentuated by the new Moon of the 22nd, when you'll certainly vow to make some permanent changes in the way you live. Are you living to work, or working to live? Your work may be at odds with your sense of self now and making the correct choices about what you want to do requires a hard trade-off perhaps.

You may think you have these problems licked by the month's end, only to find Mercury retrograde will demand further attention to them into November

Romance and Friendship

Around the fifth you'll be feeling reasonably self-satisfied. There's no reason to unsettle your inner contentedness by venturing into the crowd. An older friend may be more suited to your mood if you do prefer company.

On the 8th a lunch or café latte meeting could break down as you discover vast differences in your taste and style with that counterpart. Building up others in your mind before really getting to know them does come at a cost.

Glamour and power are your first and second names on the 10th, with the Moon moving through your Sun sign. The Sun is also favourably influencing you and this augers well for your popularity. If you dare enter a talent quest or choose to take up acting, music or other artistic interests, you'll be a winner now. Perhaps karaoke is the closest you'll get to start this time, but it certainly will be fun.

The Sun follows Mercury into Scorpio on the 23rd at the same time with Mars and Venus. You've been partying and enjoying the company of friends and lovers, only to find a dramatic shift in your attention as matters of your health and lifestyle take centre stage. If you haven't listened to your body signals, or pursued a healthy diet and daily regimen, you'll be forced to examine and work on these matters right now. As the love planet Venus enters Scorpio on the 24th, your love could obsessively grab hold of you to the exclusion of everything else. You've been putting someone on a pedestal or looking at the world through rose-coloured glasses. Around the 15th, 20th, 22nd and particularly 25th be careful to thoroughly scrutinise the "perfect" characters you come across. Some will seem too good to be true. They are!

On the domestic front things ease up as the large cluster of planets exiting your home arena provide you with a welcome release from those domestic demands. Parents born under Gemini will still need to keep their attention focused on children, especially around the 20th, when disputes and confrontations loom.

On the 21st be aware of the fact that the wrong people are noticing you at present, so offers and persistent plays being made for you by some intense individual may not be welcome. Because your love planets are edgy at this time, your emotions and focus on romantic matters within a social situation will leave you feeling strung out about someone. It may even spark a stronger reaction from you than you thought. Gracefully decline an offer. It may not be genuine.

Career and Finances

Successful negotiations ripen between the 5th and 15th. Sign your paperwork ASAP before retrograde Mercury on the 29th. Some Geminis should consider the prospect of transferring either interstate or overseas to expand their working life, since profitable karma from foreign sources is now strong. Don't procrastinate. You can have money in your hand by the seventh on the full Moon, but hedging your bets may scare off your patrons, business associates and others who wish you well at this time.

The new Moon of the 22nd is speculative and so you're likely to be bold enough to tell your employer exactly what you're thinking. That's fine, as long as you have alternative employment! Boardroom or office meetings bog down in ego clashes. Keep yours out of the pot—especially around the fourth.

The Sun in favourable aspect to Neptune on the tenth paves the way to successful litigation or other red-tape issues that have stalled over the previous month. These matters are consolidated when the planet of confusions, Neptune, moves direct on the 29th. Your doubts and confusions clear up, thank God!

The 22nd and 23rd are brilliant dates for advertising, communications, discussions and generally shaking hands on that big deal. If you're buying or selling, the Mercury and Jupiter combo is fortuitous. Sales of property, cars and other luxury items fare well under these planetary trends. Because of the full Moon falling in your profit sector, money is exceptionally good this month, which is one of the best for 2006.

Karma and Luck

This is a good time to gain some perspective on whether you

are simply seeking release from a feeling of restlessness, or if change is really warranted. Guard against hasty or rash decisions this month. Instead, proceed calmly and cautiously, trusting your inner voice to guide you. It will speak to you when you least expect it.

Carefully word your advertisement or proposal and the blessings of Mercury and Jupiter will contribute to a full bank account this month. You can successfully sell off fixed assets and be rewarded handsomely. If you possess shares or other dividend-paying investments, strong results are shown around the full Moon of the 7th and will continue to increase from here on in.

Foreign affairs, changing your place of work and even your residence give you a karmic boost now. There's a growing sense that your luck has turned the corner, with North Node and Uranus in the high part of your horoscope. At the commencement of the month a most lucky and unusual combination of Jupiter in your sixth sector and Moon in your eighth takes place. This protects you, enhances your aura, and stimulates your fortunate vibrations. Lady Luck is passing by very near to you right now.

Destiny Dates

High Times   5, 7, 8, 10, 15, 22

Tough Karma   4, 20, 21, 23

NOVEMBER

NOVEMBER

Highlights of the Month

Your sixth sector continues to influence your life and activities generally this month. This sixth sector regulates health, debts, uncles, aunts, spouse's health and even secret enemies, among other things. All of these matter in some form or another and will come into focus. Fortunately, several planets are wonderfully influenced by your finance ruler, the Moon, and whatever challenges you perceive will eventually be balanced to your benefit.

Due to an increased optimism throughout October your health is likely to improve. If there are any concerns, however small, you'll be seeking medical advice to completely alleviate them. Dietary, food, culinary and other activities associated with your sense of taste will draw your attention. Dental work may also be done.

Your daily work schedule will undergo a radical change. Maintaining your diary will be a critical component of your continued success. Changing the way you do things may be hard at first, but necessary and crucial. Don't let that fear of change affect your decision to be the best you can. On the 19th and the 21st, the planets Mercury and Uranus signal more changes that come at you hard and fast. Your preparedness with time management will ensure you pass through these transitions safely and with the deserved gains and satisfaction.

Romance and Friendship

You know, Gemini, happiness is a decision. It's not something in the future. Unhappiness is caused by the thinking mind. It's a form of laziness. So, you should attempt to forget everything sometimes, at least for a few minutes a day—even your self. Consciously forget. Say, "Yes... I am feeling happy". Did you know that even if you aren't happy, the pretence of happiness can eventually cause it to happen ? Try it. It's a form of creative visualisation in which you recollect happiness and then experience it. This very attitude will draw people to you. As a consequence a new love or romance can begin now. If the current relationship seems somewhat flat, a burst of life resurrects it. Venus transits near the new Moon of the 20th, after moving to your marriage sector on the 17th. You married Geminis may want to renew your vows, to share a deeper commitment, that commitment you have for each other during this planetary cycle.

Any tensions or moodiness with friends can be remedied by your caring and affectionate attention. Rather than pointing out the flaws in others you can encourage them lovingly by noting their better side. The previous month's idealistic energies might now have some Geminis crashing to earth in a blaze of reality. The first days of November will be especially sensitive. Your exaggerated sense of perfection swings to the opposite side: excessive negativity. Find that harmonious balance till the eighth, when normal romantic "vision" returns.

Around the 13th you may have to attend a social gathering alone. Although preparations were in place, a partner or friend may back out at the last minute. You can either accept this and enjoy the occasion or mope it out. The choice is yours.

The 15th is far better for love and social life, and feelings of jubilation fill you to the brim. Geminis working with the public or in travelling professions may meet a soul mate unexpectedly. Don't forget to exchange telephone numbers. The 17th, 22nd and 25th are going to be edgy and people's opinions and plans change like the wind. Verify with all parties the step-by-step understanding you have come to, in order to avoid any additional pressure at this time.

Domestic affairs are low key with a preference for your own quiet time around the full Moon of the 5th, as well as the 14th and 24th. The squaring of the Sun around the 17th also means you'll be looking forward to a physical "battery recharge" and laying low for at least a day or two.

Career and Finances

Levelling the financial playing field, so to speak, will be a major effort on your part this month. Consolidating your loans is uppermost in your mind, so dealing with bank managers, financial planners and advisers is not surprising, given that you're spending big just now. Expenditures may even outstrip your income, notwithstanding the lucky planetary vibrations recently. Carefully assess the situation before making rash financial moves.

Mercury and Uranus are direct on 18th and 20th respectively and cause you to falsely believe you can live a much richer lifestyle than you actually can. With Venus and Jupiter conjoined, lavish spending may continue unabated. Take note of the omens, messages and advice you receive from a friend or family confidante around the 5th, near the full Moon. The writing will be on the wall, financially speaking. Heed the advice you hear.

Positive days for money will be found on the 1st, 3rd, 8th, 16th, 26th and 28th. You could earn a little more than anticipated; back pay or forgotten overtime rates will help swell your pay envelope. At least you'll have some spare cash to deal with your escalating spending habits this month.

Around the 17th can be a very tiring and personally confusing time, when you do not know precisely what you want or you do not feel strong or effective enough to make it happen. Physically, you need to be gentle with yourself and take care not to disperse your energy reserves. Your imagination can run feral now, and you want to act out a daydream or strange desires—something you generally would have the good sense not to attempt. Tread cautiously through this fantasy day or two.

A most important development takes place on the 24th with Jupiter entering your public relations sector. You'll now be stretching your horizons as far as the eye can see and this begins a new 12-year cycle for you. Both professional and personal affairs help expand you life view and vice versa.

Karma and Luck

As Jupiter edges towards Sagittarius at the end of November, you'll notice a whole new aura surrounding you. Your world of dreams starts to materialise and luck as a whole can feel like it's following you. All your personal relationships are bolstered in a very noticeable way. Even strangers who would ordinarily pay little attention to you begin to take note, helping you to achieve your goals.

Meeting those of like mind who share your ideals and material goals is encouraging and stimulating, as the year nears an end. Your personal luck planet, Uranus, also moves forward on the 21st, and there is no doubt you'll be welcoming any element of surprise, as avant garde as it may seem in your professional arena. This is a peak month for luck all round. You'll have abundant mental energy and be eager to "attack" intellectual or conceptual problems. You are likely to come up with some clever solutions or a very workable plan, especially if you brainstorm with others. You'll also be able to make up your mind very quickly and decisively now and translate your ideas into action. If you persist confidently, you can convert these attitudes to cash.

Destiny Dates

High Times   1, 3, 8, 16, 18, 19, 20, 24, 26, 28

Tough Karma   5, 13, 14, 17, 21, 22, 25

DECEMBER

DECEMBER

Highlights of the Month

The final month of 2006 is marked by some very powerful planetary forces. The full Moon of the 5th and the new Moon of the 20th in the area of relationships are particularly notable. The powerful presence of six planets in this area and increasing strength after the 8th means you finish the year on a high note. You'll be feeling pretty good about yourself, as the seventh sector of your horoscope is very uplifting for the affairs of all these planets.

The Moon is in the area of fulfilment, wishes, friendship and financial profit at the outset of the month. Though Saturn restrains your celebrations you'll still feel an all-round satisfaction about what you've accomplished in 2006. Social interaction and a far more committed involvement are seen to permeate your upcoming life cycle. Humanitarian and philanthropic instincts will also motivate your connections with others.

Coupled with the Moon in the eleventh sector, Jupiter casting its benign glance on your friendship sector promises a higher, more polished calibre of friends, in 2007 as well. Will you even have time for work with such a busy social agenda this month, you may well ask?

The conjunction of Mercury and Mars in your sixth sector of work around the 11th is the only exception to an otherwise wonderful end to the year. Opposition from envious co-workers punches a hole in your self-confidence but your generally high optimism this month is armour enough to cause little or no long-term affect on you.

Romance and Friendship

A stellar combination of six planets in your seventh sector of the world at large is creating a backdrop of wonderful social and romantic circumstances as the year closes for you, Gemini. On the first, sharing dreams and spiritual ideas with a friend is a great idea as long as you don't allow those discussions to deteriorate into the more morose side of human nature. In doing so the second could cause you to feel depressed or withdrawn. Postpone solving your problems until a sunnier day, astrologically.

Your mind will act like a pendulum between the fourth and the seventh. Tough problems cause you to look for ways of avoiding what you realise must be dealt with. Sexual escapades in which you tempt fate won't solve your marital or romantic dilemmas. On the 8th, gossip is hot, although not necessarily true in every respect. Don't become embroiled.

Around the 8th and 9th, take the initiative in love by demanding your needs be met. Ask an attractive member of the opposite sex out for lunch or simply a long chat.

Writing a letter or receiving interesting news that requires your response is in order on the tenth. The news may or may not be positive, but it's going to grab your attention irrespective of its content.

Meeting with strangers around the 11th, 12th and 13th could prompt you to seriously consider your motives in relationship. Are money, status and other luxuries worth the sacrifice of a more solid and spiritual quality within a person? You should never marry for money. You may simply end up as an accessory for a wealthy person.

On the 17th assert your opinions. If you need to enter a debate you can do so today. Forcing an issue on the domestic front may meet with stern opposition, but your gut instincts are correct and your decision will be applauded by the following week.

On the 17th, 19th, 22nd, 23rd and 24th, others may not see you for the charmer you've become. Try to step back and see yourself through other eyes. You are more emotional on these dates and though you wish for the best socially, domestically and romantically, you'll only end up creating the opposite effect.

Notwithstanding these tough influences, a marriage proposal on the 11th is possible for some Geminis.

Career and Finances

You can round up the professional part of your life in 2006 with a sense of accomplishment. Your achievements will be boosted as Jupiter enters Sagittarius during the first week of December. Illicit the help you need from others to complete your tasks. Their assistance will act like the cherry on the cake.

Saturn's retrogression on the third will slowly move back towards a tough negotiation with Neptune. Don't begin to doubt your success or your ability, even if you must reappraise the value of what you've produced. Occasionally our first works are stepping-stones. Dreams take time to solidify and this is the meaning of the Saturn/Neptune combination.

Combative Mars enters dynamic Sagittarius. Your buoyant disposition could be tested on the 6th when this occurs. Beware of others throwing you the bait. This is a test to see how well you stand up under pressure. Mercury in Sagittarius on the eighth is conciliatory. An apology from some "evil doers" may be forthcoming and welcome by you then.

New partnerships of a business nature flourish now. Several may be in the offering. Choose solid, traditionally based directions and do so confidently after the new Moon of the 20th. You'll be severely tempted to follow the Uranus pointer towards the untested, highly risky path leading to no-man's land. Hard aspects of the Sun, Venus, Jupiter and Mars to Uranus this month cause you to be more conservative with negotiations even though the prospects seem great.

On the 10th, Mercury conjoins Jupiter in Sagittarius. Publishing that book or studying up to improve your skills is well supported by these planetary forces. There's a giant within you waiting to make its impression on the world. All activities relating to books, publishing, Internet and communications will work well for you now.

Venus moves to Capricorn on the 11th and enhances your bank balance, but also suggests an advance or gift just when you need it. The Sun and Mercury also enter Capricorn on the 22nd and the 27th respectively, bringing additional focus to money matters. Hold on to your valuables, including cash, wallet, jewellery, etc., as absentmindedness could cause loss or theft.

The final aspect of Mars to Neptune on the 31st asks you to use the greatest discrimination in the way you present your ideas. Vague or exaggerated claims should be avoided. Treat big talkers with an incredulous air.

Karma and Luck

Jupiter will lift your relationships as Venus also conjoins the combination in Sagittarius. Your opportunities for finance in December are significantly boosted. If you need money for a business venture or pet project, you'll be advanced the sum, and possibly even as a gift at that.

The likelihood of forging either permanent business ties or even marriage alliances is central to the closing chapter of 2006 for Gemini. This is where your luck and karma point to in the coming few years and where your love, enthusiasm and energies should be well directed. The quality of abundance permeates your chart, with Jupiter, Venus and the Moon, all lucky planets, attracting good karma with their beneficial blend of vibrations.

Don't stop now as the North Node and Uranus intensify their magical presence at the top of your horoscope. From here on in, anything magnificent can happen, and it probably will.

Destiny Dates

High Times   5, 9, 10, 11, 20, 22
Tough Karma   2, 6, 7, 8, 17, 19, 23, 24

YOUR 2006
PLANETARY
RULER

Each planet presides over a number between one and nine. This number, ruling your current year, predominates over your activities and the events you can expect. Here are the planets and their ruling numbers:

1 Sun, 2 Moon, 3 Jupiter, 4 Uranus, 5 Mercury, 6 Venus, 7 Neptune, 8 Saturn, 9 Mars.

By adding the numbers of your birth date and the year in question you can quickly find which planet will control the coming year for you. If, for example, you were born on 12 November, add the numbers 12 (day of birth) and 11 (month of birth) to the current year in question, that is, 2006 (current year), like this:

$1+2+1+1+2+0+0+6 = 13$.

Then add these numbers again, like this: $1+3 = 4$.

The planet ruling your individual Karma for 2006 would be Uranus.

YEAR OF THE SUN

Overview

Power, authority, light, life and popularity are the key characteristics of the Sun. This year will prove to be a blessing for you, with many successes sure to come your way. This is because these are the primary characteristics of the Sun, your ruling planet throughout 2006. These solar vibrations promise a start to new enterprises and large-scale projects. You are reinvigorated after a nine-year cycle has finished. Your health and vitality are very high and your stamina will be one of your greatest assets in this coming 12 months.

Being at the centre of the solar system the Sun will endow you with great soul force and magnetism and this means you'll be extremely popular and able to attract many new friends and lovers into your orbit. Many social opportunities, parties and outings will come your way and the only warning here is that you don't take your healthy life force for granted and waste your valuable energy.

Love and Pleasure

If you're a parent, you'll find increasing satisfaction from your family, in particular, your children. Entertainment, music, dancing and other theatrical pastimes will offer you great satisfaction. You may even decide to take up study of a musical instrument or start drama classes.

Work

Any work you commence will be successful and should you choose to move on to greener pastures, a new career move will bring you much contentment and success. Staying where you are professionally also has its benefits in a solar year: it heralds an opportunity for promotion and an increased salary as your superiors will take note of your outstanding service.

Spiritual Guidance

Good luck is more pronounced during the months of Leo, that is, August and the 1st, 8th, 15th and 22nd hours of Sunday especially will give you the edge in competition and other activities. Those born in the sign of Leo may help you or have some karmic connections with you. This is a very important year of destiny and your lucky numbers in this current cycle are 1, 10, 19 and 28. Try using gold, yellow, lemon, orange and rust colours and the lucky gemstones of garnet, red ruby and a spinel.

YEAR OF THE MOON

Overview

The emotional and receptive Moon is in control of your general affairs this year. As such you have an opportunity to re-align yourself to all of your relationships, family and domestic matters and the inner work of improving your character and mindset. The

Moon rules the number 2 and is dual or changeable in nature. You must try to be more constant in your emotional nature and decisions this year and not let your heart rule your head.

Love and Pleasure

Issues surrounding your home property and domestic affairs will be uppermost in your mind during this lunar period. If you've been postponing renovations, gardening or purchasing a new home, this could be the year in which you make your dreams come true. Relationships can be moody and emotional, though. Speak about your feelings and don't bottle them up. Men in their lunar year will be surprised at how emotional they may be. Gentlemen, if you can discuss how you feel, the women in your life will love you for it.

Work

Your work will not be as strong a focus during 2006, at least not initially. You can, however, make some important contributions to the general public and if you are independently employed, the world at large may be attracted to your offerings. In your attempts to acquire a better position, women employers and co-workers will assist you. Your intuitive sense will be strong and you can use this to tune in to opportunities that present themselves. Trust your instincts on these matters at this time.

Spiritual Guidance

Mondays generally, July—which is the month of Cancer—and the 1st, 8th, 15th and 22nd hours on Monday are very strong, as are new and full Moon days for you in this approaching year. Try to plan your affairs to coincide at these times for improved outcomes in business and personal matters. Try using the numbers 2, 11, 20 and 29 for luck and consider all the lunar objects, that is, silver, pearl, moonstone, white, and the lunar colours: cream, yellow, silver and grey. Try to steer clear of darker colours like blue and green.

YEAR OF JUPITER

Overview

The benevolent and powerful Jupiter holds sway over your life this year. Luck, expansion, wealth and popularity mark the influence of this, the largest of planets. The Jupiterian vibration has strong links with the zodiac signs of Sagittarius and Pisces and also brings out your more spiritual and compassionate nature. The deeper wealth of self-awareness and self-empowerment are very much a part of this year for you.

Love and Pleasure

As Jupiter conveys energy to you, journeys abroad may be on the cards and exploring distant lands will attract your bold and audacious mood in 2006. Mixing with people from distant lands and learning about other cultures will have a strong appeal for you and you can fulfil your desire to "travel the world".

In matters of love, Jupiter shows that you are prepared to make concessions to your partner and develop your relationships along the lines of similarities rather than differences. There can be a resurgence of feeling for your partner—or, if unattached, bright new opportunities will present themselves to you. A spiritual or karmic relationship may capture your heart in 2006.

Work

During Jupiter's year, good fortune and favours from friends, family and work associates can be expected. Should you need to approach superiors or employers for favours, they will receive you with open arms and accommodate your requests. If you're working in your own business or wish to carve out an independent path, this is the year to do it. Jupiter will bless you with abundant success and your reputation will be all the better for it.

Spiritual Guidance

Jupiter can at times exaggerate and overstep the mark. During

2006 be realistic about your plans. Expand by all means, but don't overdo it. Try not to overestimate your talents nor boast about your achievements. In social affairs, moderate your eating and drinking habits. If you must speculate, do so with good professional advice and don't be afraid to get second or even third opinions. It would also be a mistake to gamble foolishly. The Piscean energy of Jupiter will give you special spiritual insights this year. Use them to your advantage. If you are either Sagittarius or Pisces, this is particularly a good year for you. The 1st, 8th, 15th and 24th hours of Thursday will be lucky. Your lucky numbers and months are 3, 12, that is, March and December, and the numbers 21 and 30 will have a particularly good effect on you. Use the colours of yellow and ochre, and the gems yellow sapphire, golden topaz and yellow citrine for enhanced good fortune. Gold is your metal throughout 2006.

YEAR OF VENUS

Overview

If ever there was a year for love, this is it! The sensual and loving vibrations of Venus will dominate your life this year. Yes, love is definitely in the air. Venus has strong connections with the signs of Taurus and Libra, so money, love and home all feature strongly for you in 2006. For those already in committed relationships a more stabilising influence will be felt. In other cases that long-awaited marriage proposal could arrive when you least expect it! Meeting your soul mate and sharing love is your key focus this year.

Love and Pleasure

This should be a more harmonising year for your romantic affairs and can fulfil you on many levels. Meeting your soul mate is a distinct possibility, with a few added bonuses like gifts, jewellery, fashion and entertainment thrown into the mix as well. There will be several opportunities to socialise, party and generally enjoy the company of others. Try to avoid too much pleasure, though, as late nights and excessive displays of your prowess may catch up with you—sooner than you think.

Work

Stabilising your finances and looking to your long-term security, beautifying your residence and generally working towards a more financially independent lifestyle—these will be the predominating motivators this year. You'll work hard and be rewarded handsomely. Work and pleasure overlap as Venus also rules Libra, the sign of public relations, relationships and human contacts. This may turn out to be a double-edged sword as your vivacious and appealing manner will help you forge ahead, but over-socialising or a workplace love affair may backfire. Use your discretion on this one.

Spiritual Guidance

Venus has a tendency to draw your mind towards money, pleasure and generally all things materialistic. Isn't it strange how the things we love aren't supposed to be good for us (like sugar, chocolate and coffee)? There's no problem in this as long as you exercise moderation in all your activities and pay some attention to your inner and spiritual needs. By gaining a balance throughout 2006 you'll be better able to sustain your romantic and professional successes as well.

The 1st, 8th, 15th and 20th hours on a Friday will offer you lucky opportunities. Lucky numbers this year are 6, 15, 24 and 33. Cream colours, as well as white, pink and lavender will work like magic for you. Also try using diamond, white coral, zirconia and silver or platinum as favourable gems and metals this year.

YEAR OF MARS

Overview

This year is a concluding year of a nine-year-cycle and is ruled by the energetic and powerful planet Mars. How you use these vital energies at your disposal will determine just how well you commence your next cycle. As Mars is often associated with arguments, challenges and mishaps, your impulse and drive may compel you to be a little intense, causing you to fail to see the perspectives of others. This may lead to some misunderstandings or, in the extreme, lawsuits and complications in some of your relationships. By exercising a deeper level of awareness you can hopefully bypass these obstructive forces. Notwithstanding a Mars year is often very industrious and productive if you channel your energies wisely.

Love and Pleasure

Try not to be too aggravated in your relationships and friendships this year. Your pushy nature may mean well, but you could easily get others offside. A good dose of regular sport and physical activity will release your tension, thereby smoothing over your personal affairs. Outdoor activities would be a perfect form of recreation during this Mars cycle. Nature and fresh air, hobbies and social engagements will give you great satisfaction.

Work

Your health and vitality are extremely high this year and so no task or duty will be insurmountable. In fact, you may border on "workaholic" mode and will need to check the tendency to overwork. You will achieve an enormous amount and forge ahead professionally. Remember quality, not quantity, is the name of the game and by producing good work your reputation will grow. Cross your t's and dot your i's and you'll create a solid foundation for the coming solar cycle. You'll also be lucky in property purchases, building and construction.

Spiritual Guidance

Some form of mental peace or meditation would be helpful in 2006 to bring the heat down. Even if you're in some dispute, you might want to try a more reconciliatory approach rather than a confrontational attitude. This would further augment and create positive influences on your health and relations generally.

The 1st, 8th, 15th and 20th hours of Tuesday are lucky this year. If you do need to litigate or attend to health matters these intervals on a Tuesday are beneficial. Your lucky numbers are 9, 18, 27 and 36. Red coral and garnet are the gems of Mars and will enhance your luck. Red and autumn tones as well as crimson are your best fashion colours in 2006.

YEAR OF MERCURY

Overview

The secret to your success this year is communication. As your yearly ruling planet is the sharp and intellectual Mercury, all forms of written and spoken speech will be the key to you getting ahead. Your imagination should soar and you'll be filled with unique and exciting ideas. There should be no fear in making proposals, applying for new jobs, resolving differences with others or signing contracts. You have to be very decisive as many chances coming your way could confuse you and create doubt.

Love and Pleasure

In your closest relationships this year you may find yourself in two minds. As Mercury rules Gemini in Virgo, it is a dual, changeable and critical planet. You'll blow hot and cold, feeling intense love on the one hand and enormous aversion on the other. Your critical nature might alienate those you love most. There's a vast difference between constructive criticism and persistent attention to others' weaknesses. Work on your own self and encourage others' strengths and talents..This will work wonders for your love life throughout 2006.

Work

Your employment circumstances could change this year. Either the office environment in which you work or the way you do things will be subject to a long overdue overhaul. It may be you who takes the initiative to create a more harmonious work environment for yourself. Your work this year could involve travel or at least a lot more interaction with the public as a whole. There may be some requirement on your part to improve your skills through study or supplementary courses. Make sure you're in the right sort of career or the extra commitment required could frazzle you if you're short on time.

Spiritual Guidance

Every effort should be made to keep your mind and heart steady. There will be an overload of information, paperwork, messages and day-to-day contacts. Can you manage all this? Your schedules and time management will have to be extremely well executed. This being the case, you can focus entirely on the ideas and success that 2006 will bring. Eat well and supplement your diet with herbs and vitamins. An overall check-up with your GP should augment your health. The 1st, 8th, 15th and 20th hours of a Wednesday are lucky hours and for important meetings and events you should schedule these times in your diary. Green emerald, aquamarine, green peridot or jade will enhance your aura and general prospects this year, and this will be more the case if you use the lucky numbers of 5, 14, 23 and 32. All shades of green are very lucky fashion statements in 2006.

YEAR OF SATURN

Overview

Throughout history people have feared Saturn, but this is due to an ongoing ignorance of the beneficial side of this planet. In fact, Saturn is the principal giver of karma and deserved fortune and will bless you in its ruling year. During 2006 Saturn controls the affairs of your life and if you are prepared and able to work with the discipline and practical demands that these vibrations bring, you can achieve great mental and financial successes in the coming twelve months. The planet Saturn resonates most closely with the star sign of Capricorn—a practical, material and ambitious energy. By attuning yourself to Saturn you can achieve your ambitions slowly but surely in a diligent way.

Love and Pleasure

Will you have time for romance in 2006? That's the question. With your work commitments loved ones may feel you're ignoring them and giving undue weight to your career life. Your diplomatic skills will be called upon to work this one out as you walk the work/love tightrope throughout the year. Your partner or some family member could have their own problems that may fall on your shoulders. Yet another responsibility Saturn brings in its wake! Your recreation may even seem like hard work as you find it difficult to unwind this year. Spend some time doing nothing on the odd weekend as it will make a world of difference to you and offer you some peace of mind during this challenging cycle.

Work

The number 8 is considered financially lucky by the Chinese. This could have something to do with the affinity of the number 8 and its ruler Saturn. In 2006 these financial and economic concerns and activities become paramount in your life. There will be heavier responsibilities this year but you're likely to take them on, if only to prove to yourself you are capable of handling what life dishes up. As a result, promotions of a high order are on the way. Saturn may test you with laborious and repetitive tasks so don't think the predicted promotion is a ticket to freedom—not just yet. Your hard work will pay off and the remuneration in 2006 will be a welcome return for your sacrifices.

Spiritual Guidance

Use caution in your dealings this year and speak sparingly. Try not to let negative thoughts undermine your excellent efforts and don't be afraid to give yourself a pat on the back for your successes. Love and honour yourself this year. Those born in Capricorn and Aquarius are particularly lucky this year and on Saturdays during the 1st, 8th, 15th and 20th hours of the day exceptionally good luck may be expected. Blue, purple and black colours are lucky as are blue sapphire, amethyst and lapis lazuli. All shades of blue will enhance your aura in this, the year of Saturn.

YEAR OF URANUS

Overview

Uranus is always surprising, sudden and dramatic in its actions and effects. 2006 will be dominated by this most electrifying and exciting planet. Surprising and unexpected results are likely in both your personal and professional life. In this year ruled by Uranus you will venture to attempt things you had only previously dreamed of doing. You'll break down the barriers of your self-limitations and challenge your family and social traditions, if this is what is needed, to gain your independence and spiritual freedom. Aquarius is ruled by Uranus (the North Node or Karma Point of the zodiac is also an additional factor this year and promises a progressive and inspiring cycle for you).

Work

Uranus is a technological planet. If you have avoided incorporating electronics, new media and computing equipment in your career in the past, it may be unavoidable this year. You'll be challenged to "get with the program" and modernise your system of doing things. You'll be much busier in 2006 so an open mind to this progressive technology will prove to be a blessing in disguise as it will ultimately make you more efficient and save you loads of time. New friends and alliances will be formed through your profession, as Aquarius is the New Age humanitarian sign of friendship. Positive surprises through work and co-workers can be expected.

Love and Pleasure

During this year you'll attempt to change the status quo in your relationships. If your love life has become stale and uninspiring, you could take drastic steps to make a new start. This could be triggered through the chance meeting of unusual people to whom you feel a past karmic connection. It will be hard to resist that temptation to try something new. Remember, though, the grass isn't necessarily greener on the other side.

Spiritual Guidance

Exercise patience this year and don't react impulsively to situations or people who seem to offer you a brand new life. Promises may be short on delivery. Carefully discriminate and assess new opportunities socially, romantically or professionally. Those born under Aquarius or in November, that is, Scorpio, can be exceptionally lucky this year. The 1st, 8th, 15th and 20th hours of Saturday are lucky, although luck will knock on your door when you least expect it throughout 2006. That is the nature of Uranus. Iridescent, electric and mixed colours are auspicious and amethyst, hessonite, garnet and opal, especially of a blue colour, are your gems of fortune this year.

YEAR OF NEPTUNE

Overview

Neptune has an affinity with the zodiac sign of Pisces, the twelfth and final horoscope sector. This is a spiritual, idealistic and sensitive sign that can accelerate your evolution on the one hand or, at the other extreme, can confuse and disorientate. Depending on your level of understanding, 2006 will either propel you forward to your next cycle or you may have some important unfinished karmic business to attend to: Your character, psychological and emotional issues will come to the fore and how you deal with these aspects of your life will determine the extent of your successes in the coming 12 months.

Love and Pleasure

Don't be too trusting of those who wish to take advantage of you in this cycle. Someone may sweep you off your feet and hypnotise you with their charm, but ask the question, "What is their underlying motive?" Be a step ahead of anyone you meet by keeping your wits about you. You have big dreams in your romantic life so just make sure you take the rose-coloured glasses off before looking at the world in this cycle of Neptune. If you're realistic you may well meet a kindred spirit, someone who may be your long-awaited soul mate.

Work

As Neptune signifies sacrifice, you'll be called on to make some extra effort in work. People you work with will require your assistance and guidance, which means you may have to postpone your own goals and ambitions for now. Family members may have their own challenges and will call upon you to go the extra mile for them at the expense of your own achievement. Try to develop clarity in your goals this year as confusion over the type of work you wish to do may surface. You have to be ruthlessly honest about your life mission and ask yourself, "Is this the work I really want to do?" A choice between money, security, creativity and inspiration is at the heart of your professional decisions in 2006.

Spiritual Guidance

By meditation, introspection and careful self-analysis, you can become a great person. This is a year of self-empowerment when all forms of self-victimisation are dropped. Social work, charity, community service and spiritual idealism are all strongly marked for you. Believe it or not, these activities will result in positive material benefits for you. That is the law of karma. The 1st, 8th, 15th and 20th hours of Tuesday provide lucky energy. Those born in Pisces are very fortunate as are those born in July, that is, Cancer. Wear red colours; ash and grey tones will also attract good fortune to you. Cat's-eye chrysoberyl and turquoise are your lucky gems throughout the year of Neptune in 2006.

YOUR DAILY

PLANNER

There is a lesser known branch of astrology called Electional Astrology, which can guide us in selecting the most appropriate times to conduct our day-to-day affairs of life. The ancient astrologers were fully aware of the planetary patterns and how they impacted each of us. Knowing of these outcomes in advance gave them the opportunity to suggest the best possible times to commence important activities. This was, and continues to be a popular practice with modern farmers who, understanding the phases of the Moon, attest to the fact that planting seeds on certain lunar days produces a far superior crop. In your personal almanac we revive the practice called Electional Astrology so that you can choose an activity and be sure that the planetary energies will be in sync with you, offering the best possible outcome. Coupled with knowledge of your monthly and weekly trends, the almanac becomes a powerful tool for capitalising on opportunities throughout the year.

The following section covers many different areas of day-to-day life. Using the different cycles of the Moon and the combined strength of the other planets, you'll be able to quickly and very simply scan the year for the best times on which to start the activity you have in mind. Simply select the activity and the likely month and fine-tune your timing by noting the best dates. The almanac specifically chooses the best Lunar times and aggregate planetary aspects to arrive at these dates. Good luck and may the planets bless you with great success, fortune and happiness!

COMMENCING DIFFERENT ACTIVITIES

How many times have we made that New Year's resolution to begin a diet or lose weight or to be a better person in our relationships, etc? Well, commencing different activities and the success and outcome of those activities is indeed strongly influenced by the Lunar and planetary positions. The following activities should be commenced on the days as indicated.

HEALTH AND HEALING

To start a diet

January	15, 16, 17, 18, 19, 25, 26, 29
February	13, 14, 15, 21, 22, 25, 26
March	20, 21, 22, 25, 26
April	17, 18, 21, 22, 25, 26
May	14, 15, 18, 19, 23, 24
June	15, 16, 19, 20
July	12, 13, 16, 17
August	13, 21, 22, 23
September	9, 10, 18, 19, 20, 21
October	7, 15, 16, 17, 18, 19
November	11, 12, 13, 14, 15
December	10, 11, 12, 18, 19, 20

To make a medical or dental appointment

January	1, 2, 3, 4, 5, 8, 11, 12, 13, 14, 15, 16, 17, 19, 20, 21, 22, 23, 24, 28
February	1, 21, 23, 24
March	20, 22, 23, 24, 25, 26, 27, 28, 29, 30, 31
April	1, 2, 3, 9, 11, 12, 13, 14, 15, 16, 17, 18, 19, 20, 21, 22, 23, 24, 25, 26, 27, 29

May	2, 3, 4, 5, 6, 8, 9, 10, 13, 14, 15, 16, 17, 18, 19, 20, 21, 22, 23, 24, 26, 28, 29, 30, 31
June	1, 2, 10, 15, 16, 17, 18, 19, 20, 21
July	9, 10, 11, 12, 13, 14, 15, 16, 17, 18, 19, 20, 23, 24, 25, 26, 27, 29
August	4, 5, 6, 7, 8, 9, 10, 11, 12, 15, 25, 26, 27, 28, 29, 30, 31
September	10, 12, 13, 15
October	7, 8, 9, 10, 11, 12, 13, 14, 15, 16, 17, 19, 20, 21, 22, 23, 24, 25, 26, 27, 28, 29, 30, 31
November	1, 2, 5, 6, 9, 10, 11, 12, 13, 14, 15, 16, 17, 18, 19, 20, 21, 22, 23, 24, 27, 29, 30
December	1, 2, 3, 5, 6, 7, 8, 9, 10, 11, 12, 13, 14, 15, 20, 21, 27, 28, 29, 30, 31

FINANCIAL MATTERS

To open a savings account

January	1, 8, 9
February	4, 5
March	3, 4, 5, 31
April	1, 28
May	12
June	8, 9

July	5, 6, 7, 10
August	2, 3, 6, 7, 29, 30
September	3, 4, 25, 26, 27, 30
October	1, 22, 23, 24, 27, 28
November	5, 23, 24, 25
December	2, 3, 21, 22, 29, 30

To start a new venture

January	1, 2, 3, 4, 5, 6, 7, 8, 9, 10, 11, 12, 13, 30, 31
February	1, 2, 3, 4, 5, 6, 7, 8, 9, 10, 11, 12
March	1, 2, 3, 4, 5, 6, 7, 8, 9, 10, 11, 12, 13, 14, 29, 30
April	1, 2, 3, 4, 5, 6, 7, 8, 9, 10, 11, 12, 13, 28, 29, 30
May	1, 2, 3, 4, 5, 6, 7, 8, 9, 10, 11, 12, 27, 28, 29, 30, 31
June	1, 2, 3, 4, 5, 6, 7, 8, 9, 10, 11, 26, 27, 28, 29, 30
July	1, 2, 3, 4, 5, 6, 7, 8, 9, 10, 25, 26, 27, 28, 29, 30, 31
August	1, 2, 3, 4, 5, 6, 7, 8, 24, 25, 26, 27, 28, 29, 30, 31
September	1, 2, 3, 4, 5, 6, 7, 22, 23, 24, 25, 26, 27, 28, 29, 30
October	1, 2, 3, 4, 5, 6, 22, 23, 24, 25, 26, 27, 28, 29, 30, 31
November	1, 2, 3, 4, 5, 21, 22, 23, 24, 25, 26, 27, 28, 29, 30
December	1, 2, 3, 4, 21, 22, 23, 24, 25, 26, 27, 28, 29, 30, 31

To purchase property

January	2, 3, 8, 9, 15, 16, 22, 23, 24, 29, 30
February	4, 5, 11, 12, 13, 19, 20, 25, 26
March	3, 4, 5, 10, 11, 12, 18, 19, 25, 26, 31
April	1, 7, 8, 14, 15, 16, 21, 22, 27, 28
May	4, 5, 6, 12, 13, 18, 19, 25, 26, 31

June	1, 2, 8, 9, 15, 16, 21, 22, 28, 29
July	5, 6, 7, 12, 13, 18, 19, 25, 26
August	2, 3, 8, 9, 14, 15, 16, 21, 22, 23, 29, 30
September	5, 6, 11, 12, 18, 19, 25, 26, 27
October	2, 3, 8, 9, 15, 16, 22, 23, 24, 29, 30, 31
November	5, 6, 11, 12, 13, 19, 20, 26, 27
December	2, 3, 8, 9, 10, 16, 17, 23, 24, 29, 30

To purchase cars and other machinery

January	1, 2, 3, 4, 5, 8, 11, 12, 13, 14, 15, 16, 17, 18, 19, 20, 21, 22, 23, 24, 25, 28
February	5, 14, 21, 23, 24, 28
March	6, 11, 16, 17, 20, 21, 22, 23, 24, 25, 26, 27, 28, 29, 30, 31
April	1, 2, 3, 4, 5, 10, 11, 14, 15, 16, 17, 18, 19, 20, 21, 22, 23, 24, 28, 30
May	2, 3, 4, 5, 6, 7, 8, 9, 10, 11, 12, 13, 14, 26
June	4, 10, 11, 12, 13, 15, 16, 17, 18, 19, 20, 21
July	5, 6, 7, 8, 10, 11, 12, 13, 14, 15, 16, 17, 18
August	4, 10, 11, 12, 15, 17, 21
September	1, 2, 3, 4, 5, 6, 7, 8, 9, 14, 15, 16, 17, 18, 19
October	7, 8, 9, 10, 11, 12, 13, 14, 15, 16, 17, 18, 19, 20, 21, 22, 23, 24, 25, 26, 27, 28, 29, 30, 31
November	1, 2, 3, 4, 5, 6, 7, 9, 10, 11, 12, 13, 14, 19, 20, 25, 26, 27, 28, 29
December	1, 2, 3, 4, 5, 6, 7, 8, 9, 10, 11, 12, 13, 14, 15, 19, 20, 21, 22, 28

To conduct stock market transactions

January	1, 6, 7, 12, 13, 14, 20, 21, 27, 28
February	2, 3, 9, 10, 16, 23, 24
March	1, 2, 8, 9, 15, 16, 17, 23, 24, 29, 30
April	4, 5, 6, 12, 13, 19, 20, 25, 26
May	2, 3, 9, 10, 11, 16, 17, 23, 24, 29, 30
June	5, 6, 7, 12, 13, 14, 19, 20, 25, 26, 27
July	3, 4, 10, 11, 16, 17, 23, 24, 30, 31
August	1, 6, 7, 12, 13, 19, 20, 26, 27, 28
September	3, 4, 9, 10, 15, 16, 17, 23, 24, 30
October	1, 6, 7, 12, 13, 14, 20, 21, 27, 28
November	3, 4, 9, 10, 16, 17, 18, 23, 24, 25, 30
December	1, 6, 7, 13, 14, 15, 21, 22, 27, 28

To sell things

January	2, 3, 4, 5, 6, 7, 8, 9, 10, 11, 12, 13, 14, 15, 16, 17, 18, 19, 20, 21, 22, 23, 24, 25, 26, 27, 28, 29, 30, 31
February	1, 2, 3, 4, 5, 6, 7, 8, 9, 10, 11, 12, 13, 14, 15, 16, 17, 18, 19, 20, 21, 22, 23, 24, 25, 26, 27, 28
March	1, 2, 3, 4, 5, 7, 11, 12, 13, 14, 15, 16, 17, 18, 19, 20, 21, 22, 23, 24, 25, 26, 27, 28, 29, 30
April	1, 2, 3, 4, 5, 6, 10, 11, 15, 16, 18, 19, 20, 21, 28
May	1, 2, 3, 4, 5, 6, 7, 8, 9, 10, 11, 12, 13, 14, 15, 16, 20, 21, 22, 26, 28, 30
June	8, 10, 15, 16, 17, 18, 19, 20, 21
July	10, 11, 13, 14, 15, 16, 17, 18
August	3, 4, 12, 21, 22, 23

September	2, 3, 4, 5, 8, 15, 26
October	5, 7, 8, 9, 10, 13, 15, 16, 17, 18, 19, 20, 21, 22, 23, 24, 25, 26, 27, 28, 29, 30, 31
November	1, 2, 3, 4, 6, 9, 10, 11, 12, 13, 14, 19, 20, 24
December	3, 4, 5, 6, 7, 8, 9, 10, 11, 12, 13, 14, 15, 18, 19, 20, 21, 23, 25, 28

To borrow money

January	11, 22, 23, 24, 27, 28
February	19, 20, 23, 24
March	18, 19, 23, 24
April	14, 15, 19, 20
May	13, 16, 17
June	12, 13, 14, 25
July	11, 23, 24
August	19, 20
September	15, 16, 17
October	12, 13, 14
November	9, 10, 19, 20
December	6, 7, 16, 17

To write a will

January	
February	
March	3, 10
April	1
May	

June	8
July	
August	2, 29, 30
September	25, 26
October	22, 23, 24, 29, 30, 31
November	5, 26
December	3, 23, 24

CAREER AND STUDY

To commence education

January	10, 11
February	6, 7, 8
March	6, 7, 13, 14
April	2, 3, 9, 10, 11, 29, 30
May	1, 7, 8, 27, 28
June	3, 4, 10, 11, 30
July	1, 2, 8, 9, 27, 28, 29
August	4, 5, 24, 25, 31
September	1, 2, 22, 28, 29
October	25, 26
November	21, 22

| December | 4, 31 |

To apply for a promotion

January	12, 13, 14, 19, 22, 31
February	1, 2, 3, 6, 7, 8, 9, 10, 12, 14, 20
March	4, 5, 7, 16, 17, 19, 21
April	1, 2, 3, 4, 5, 6, 15, 16
May	12, 13, 15, 16, 19, 20, 28, 30
June	1, 2
July	19, 20, 21, 23, 24, 25, 26, 28, 29, 30, 31
August	22, 23
September	3, 5, 24, 25, 26, 29
October	
November	24
December	

To start a new job

January	1, 8, 9
February	4, 5
March	3, 4, 5, 13, 14, 15, 31
April	1, 9, 10, 11, 28
May	7, 8
June	3, 4, 30
July	1, 2, 10, 27, 28, 29
August	6, 7, 24, 25
September	3, 4, 22, 30
October	1, 27, 28

| November | 5, 23, 24, 25 |
| December | 2, 3, 21, 22, 29, 30 |

To join an organisation

January	2, 3, 10, 11, 20, 21, 29, 30
February	6, 7, 8, 16, 17, 18, 25, 26
March	6, 7, 15, 16, 17, 25, 26
April	2, 3, 12, 13, 21, 22, 29, 30
May	1, 9, 10, 11, 18, 19, 27, 28
June	5, 6, 7, 15, 16, 23, 24
July	3, 4, 12, 13, 20, 21, 22, 30, 31
August	1, 8, 9, 17, 18, 26, 27, 28
September	5, 6, 13, 14, 23, 24
October	2, 3, 10, 11, 20, 21, 29, 30, 31
November	7, 8, 16, 17, 18, 26, 27
December	4, 5, 13, 14, 15, 23, 24, 31

PERSONAL RELATIONSHIPS

One of the most important aspects of life is the selection of the right people with whom we'd like to spend our social time and possibly, if the compatibility is great, that soul mate or partner with whom we'd like to spend the rest of our lives. The daily planner looks at the best possible times for meeting friends, involving yourself in relationships, creating partnerships and even selecting appropriate dates for marriage.

Meeting friends

January	
February	
March	6, 25, 26
April	2, 3, 21, 22, 30
May	1, 19, 27
June	15, 16
July	12, 13
August	17
September	5, 6, 14
October	29, 30, 31
November	7, 8, 26
December	5

Marriage

January	4, 5, 8, 9, 12, 13, 31
February	1, 4, 5, 9, 10, 11, 12, 28
March	3, 10
April	1, 28
May	2, 3, 4, 5, 6, 9, 10, 11, 29
June	5, 6, 7, 26, 27, 28, 29
July	3, 25, 26, 30, 31
August	1, 26
September	7, 23

October	4, 5
November	1, 2, 5
December	29, 20

Romance—in a long-term relationship

January	4, 5, 8, 9, 12, 13, 31
February	1, 4, 5, 9, 10, 11, 12, 28
March	3, 10
April	1, 28
May	2, 3, 4, 5, 6, 9, 10, 11, 29
June	5, 6, 7, 26, 27, 28, 29
July	3, 25, 26, 30, 31
August	1, 26
September	7, 23
October	4, 5
November	1, 2, 5
December	29, 30

Romance—in a short-term relationship

January	6, 7
February	2, 3
March	29, 30
April	
May	
June	
July	
August	

September	
October	
November	3, 4
December	

Ending a romance

January	14, 17, 18, 19, 20, 21, 25, 26, 27, 28
February	14, 15, 16, 17, 18, 21, 22, 23, 24, 27
March	15, 16, 17, 20, 21, 22, 23, 24, 27, 28
April	17, 18, 19, 20, 23, 24, 25, 26
May	14, 15, 16, 17, 20, 21, 22, 23, 24
June	12, 13, 14, 17, 18, 19, 20, 23, 24, 25
July	11, 14, 15, 16, 17, 20, 21, 22, 23, 24
August	10, 11, 12, 13, 17, 18, 19, 20
September	8, 9, 10, 13, 14, 15, 16, 17, 20, 21
October	7, 10, 11, 12, 13, 14, 17, 18, 19, 20, 21
November	7, 8, 9, 10, 14, 15, 16, 17, 18
December	5, 6, 7, 11, 12, 13, 14, 15, 18, 19, 20

Throwing a party

January	10, 11, 15, 16, 21
February	6, 7, 8, 11, 12, 13, 16, 17, 18
March	10, 15, 16, 17, 25, 26
April	2, 3, 21, 22
May	1, 9, 11, 19
June	1, 6, 7, 15, 16, 28, 29
July	13, 20, 21, 25, 26, 30, 31

August	22, 23, 26
September	5, 6, 18, 19
October	15, 16, 20, 21, 29, 30, 31
November	13, 16, 17
December	8, 9

BEAUTY AND GROOMING

The selection of appropriate times for beautifying oneself goes far deeper than a level of superficiality. According to astrology the electromagnetic and subtle energies that are contained within our bodies are also emanating through such things as our hair and our fingernails. This is why on a cold, windy night sparks can be seen coming off your body when you take your woollen clothing off in a dark room. This being the case, astrology declares that at different times of the month and under certain planetary positions, forces will produce an increase of electrostatic discharge from the body. To minimise the loss of energy through such things as hair-cutting and the cutting of fingernails, it's best to perform these activities on days that are not going to deplete your vital energy. The following dates are excellent to not only look your best, but to feel great as well.

Buying clothes and fashion accessories

January	31
February	1, 2, 3, 6, 7, 8, 9, 28
March	1, 2, 3, 4, 5, 7, 29, 30

April	1, 2, 3
May	1, 2, 3, 4, 5, 6, 9, 12, 27, 28, 30
June	6, 8
July	28, 30, 31
August	1, 2, 3, 8
September	3, 4, 5
October	22, 23, 24, 25, 26, 27, 28, 29, 30, 31
November	1, 2, 3, 4, 24
December	

Haircuts

January	4, 5, 10, 11, 12, 25, 26, 31
February	1, 6, 7, 8, 21, 22, 27, 28
March	6, 7, 20, 21, 22, 27, 28
April	2, 3, 17, 18, 23, 24, 29, 30
May	1, 14, 15, 20, 21, 22, 27, 28
June	10, 11, 17, 18, 23, 24
July	8, 9, 14, 15, 20, 21, 22
August	4, 5, 10, 11, 17, 18, 31
September	1, 2, 7, 8, 13, 14, 28, 29
October	4, 5, 10, 11, 25, 26
November	1, 2, 7, 8, 21, 22, 28, 29
December	4, 5, 18, 19, 20, 25, 26, 31

Beauty treatments

| January | 2, 3, 8, 9, 12, 13, 14, 15, 16, 20, 21, 22, 23, 24, 29, 30 |
| February | 5, 9, 10, 11, 12, 13, 16, 17, 18, 19, 20 |

March	3, 8, 9, 10, 11, 12, 15, 16, 17, 18, 19, 25, 26, 31
April	1, 4, 5, 6, 15, 21, 22, 28
May	2, 3, 4, 5, 6, 9, 10, 11, 12, 13, 19, 25, 26
June	5, 6, 7, 8, 9, 15, 16, 21, 27, 28, 29
July	3, 5, 12, 13, 31
August	2, 3, 14, 21, 22, 23, 26, 27, 28, 29, 30
September	5, 6, 11, 16, 17, 18, 19, 26
October	3, 8, 9, 12, 13, 14, 15, 16, 17, 20, 21, 22, 23, 24, 29, 30, 31
November	5, 6, 9, 10, 11, 12, 13, 16, 17, 18, 19, 20, 26
December	6, 7, 8, 9, 10, 13, 14

Cosmetic and plastic surgery

January	5, 6, 7, 9, 10, 11, 12, 13, 31
February	1, 2, 3, 8, 9, 10, 11, 12, 28
March	1, 2, 3, 4, 5, 6, 7, 29, 30
April	1, 2, 3, 4, 6, 7, 8, 9, 10, 11, 12, 28, 29, 30
May	1, 2, 3, 4, 5, 6, 9, 11, 12, 27, 28, 29, 30, 31
June	1, 2, 3, 9, 10, 26, 27, 28, 29
July	8, 9, 10, 25, 26, 27, 28, 29, 30, 31
August	1, 3, 5, 6, 7, 8, 24, 25, 26
September	22, 23, 24, 25, 26, 27, 28, 29
October	1, 2, 3, 4, 5, 6, 22, 23, 24, 25, 26, 27, 28, 29, 30, 31
November	1, 2, 3, 4, 21, 22, 23, 24
December	21, 22

HOME

Repairs and maintenance

January	15, 16, 22, 23, 24, 29
February	13, 19, 20, 25, 26
March	18, 19, 25, 26
April	14, 15, 16, 21, 22, 27
May	13, 18, 19, 25, 26
June	15, 16, 21, 22
July	12, 13, 18, 19
August	9, 14, 15, 16, 22, 23
September	11, 12, 18, 19
October	8, 9, 15, 16
November	6, 11, 12, 13, 19, 20
December	8, 9, 10, 16, 17

Painting

January	15, 16, 22, 23, 24, 29
February	13, 19, 20, 25, 26
March	18, 19, 25, 26
April	14, 15, 16, 21, 22, 27
May	13, 18, 19, 25, 26

June	15, 16, 21, 22
July	12, 13, 18, 19
August	9, 14, 15, 16, 22, 23
September	11, 12, 18, 19
October	8, 9, 15, 16
November	6, 11, 12, 13, 19, 20
December	8, 9, 10, 16, 17

To commence building, construction and renovation

January	
February	
March	
April	
May	18, 19
June	15, 16
July	
August	9, 15
September	
October	8, 9
November	6, 11, 12
December	8, 9, 10

SUBSCRIBE TO MIRA TODAY *AND TAKE ONE BOOK FREE!*

FREE

Enjoy one FREE MIRA book when you agree to trial a MIRA subscription with our home delivery service.

PLUS: you'll also receive a <u>FREE</u> mystery gift just for giving us a try!

By subscribing to Mira you'll enjoy:

✓ The convenience of books delivered to your door every month

✓ Savings off the cover price every month

✓ Exclusive Competitions, Free Gifts, Author News, and much, much more

✓ Friendly Customer Service Team to answer your calls

✓ No Obligation, No Minimum Number of Purchases—No Risk at All!

It's so easy! Mail this coupon FREE to: Harlequin Enterprises
**Reply Paid 63360, CHATSWOOD NSW 2067. *FREE POSTAGE AND HANDLING*

-------------------- **NO STAMP REQUIRED** -------------- ✂

Yes! Please send me one FREE MIRA PLUS my <u>FREE</u> mystery gift. Then send me 2 brand-new books every month delivered directly to my door. Bill me at the low price of just $11.80 per book—that's a total price of $23.60* including GST. That's the complete price, and if I wish to cancel my subscription all I have to do is write or call Harlequin Enterprises within 10 days. I understand that accepting the book and gift places me under no obligation ever to buy any books- they are mine to keep forever. Plus, my MIRA subscription is completely flexible- I can always return a shipment, suspend or cancel at any time. I am over 18 years of age.

*Your FREE book may differ from the one pictured above

Mrs/Ms/Miss/Mr_____ AZS5HS
                                        PLEASE PRINT

Account number (if known)_____

Address _____

_____ P/code _____

Daytime Tele. No. (_____)_____

Signature_____

adma
DIRECT MARKETING
CODE COMPLIANT

APPROVED TRADER
NZ DIRECT MARKETING ASSOCIATION

10 PULASAN ROAD

#X01 - 06 GALLERY 8

SINGAPORE

424 37 8

HOME # (65)- 6348 3524